D
NT

ROD BENSON

Are you ready for a better life?

CONTENTS

Sorry it took so long. I was busy being an athlete.

INTRODUCTION

Unless you were fully tapped into the NBA blog scene of the mid 2000's, you're unlikely to know me. My name is Rodrique Benson and I played basketball for a living for a long time and for free for a lot of years, too.

I made money, lost money, made friends, lost them, fell in and out of love, gave an unfathomable amount of buckets, and everything in between. I've played organized games in places you had to drive through the jungle to get to. Man, I've sat through an entire half of basketball while a woman blew a vuvuzela into my ear just to be an asshole. All these wild experiences, and I was still just the average professional basketball player. But who wants to read about an average guy?

I ask that because our stories are told in ways that were once cool, but now feel odd. In fact, when I was asked what kind of book I wanted to write, my first response was "not a memoir." This wasn't because I'm anti memoir or the folks that write them, but because of how conditioned we are to the sports memoir.

I feel like the average sports memoir is about some guy who lived a life so amazing that most of the stories are inaccessible to the average person. These stories aren't bad, but they're for fans. It's one person reminding an audience how great they once were.

Of course there is an appetite for that at times. I would happily read everything about Tiger Woods or Michael Jordan, if they wrote it. But they don't. If they did, that book would likely be so legendary that there might be a cultural shift.

That's not to say that a memoir written by Jud Beuchler wouldn't be interesting, it just couldn't tell the same story the same way as Michal Jordan. Unfortunately, though, most memoirs, whether written by a Hall of Famer or a guy who played nine seasons among four teams, have a similar formula. The author remembers certain linear events, gives some background about what needed to be overcome (sex, drugs, teammates, death, military service) and then lists the lessons learned from said achievements.

It's really not a bad formula! But for me, once you get past Rodman and Aggasi, the stories don't hit the same. I feel like if I wrote *that* book, I myself wouldn't want to read it. What was so important about my career as a basketball player that you just *must* read about it? Nothing. Well, nothing if you're looking for stories about human achievement.

But, call me crazy, the further I get away from my career, the less I care about any of the achievements. That's not to say that the wins and losses didn't matter, it's to say I can now firmly say they never really mattered in the end. The experience as a whole is what mattered. And that experience goes way beyond sex, drugs, and a life lesson.

Different Dude isn't a book that gets spicy. Well, it does get spicy at times, but the spice is never the point. Some of the names are changed, and I won't say which. So don't ask. This isn't about exposing anyone or anything. This is a collection of stories told in random order, about things no one usually discusses, because their audience has never asked for it. Maybe they have never asked for it because the process to create a book is so formulaic that every beat from the production to the consumption is expected. I bet some of you are even surprised that the cover doesn't say "with (insert famous journalist here)."

But I don't have a ghost writer. I hardly have an audience anymore, given how long it's been since I played. What I do have are stories that tell the truth. Stories that remind us that basketball is just a job and that job came with growing pains, confusion, laughter, tears, and occasionally an 8 footer from a country you've never been to. No, really. The dude from Rush Hour elbowed me in the face.

What I aim to do with DD isn't to tell you about a life you didn't live, but to invite you into a club you've never been inside of so you can decide if it's as cool as advertised. It's people doing regular-people things, but occasionally placing a jersey over their chest beforehand.

I hope that when you finish the book, the overwhelming feeling isn't "I wish I could have done that," but instead "I really could have done that. It would have gone similarly."

I want to give the actual answer to the question "what if I had your height?"

This isn't, as most hoops books go, a 'love letter to basketball.' This isn't a haters guide to a basketball career, either. It's more like a collection of letters, written by a widower about his imperfect marriage to someone he can hardly remember without photographs anymore.

There's another important note. I finished this book a month ago and have been editing it and revising since. Last night Derek (my favorite editor at SFGATE) and I spoke about this book project. I told him it was ready-ready.

"It hasn't had a line edit," he said.

"No, but that's next an–" I started before he rolled his eyes.

"If it doesn't have a line edit yet then it's not close. You can't put out a book without a line edit."

I led with 'favorite' editor because he is. We have become very close over the last decade and I'm proud to call him a friend. I don't bring him up to bash him. I bring him up because, as a columnist, I've learned a lot about what edits mean.

When I started at Yahoo!, I didn't care about the edits. I would submit my word jumble, expecting it to be poorly written (it was) and that the powers that be would clean it up. 15 years later and I was at SFGATE behaving the same way. That's not a bad thing. I generally respect and love the people I work with, so when they return an edit, I won't even read it most of the time. I'm sure it's good.

There was one exception.

I was writing about Draymond Green and his comments about Boston fans being racist. I'd never experienced racism in Boston personally, so I did some research to see if I could make his case for him. What I found was that in 2014, PK Subban received thousands of tweets containing the N-word after beating the Bruins in a playoff game. I listed them as follows:

— That stupid n***** doesn't belong in hockey #whitesonly

— F*** YOU N***** SUBBAN YOU BELONG IN A F****** HOLE NOT AN ICE RINK

— PK Subban = F****** N*****

— F*** PK Subban. F****** n*****. Wish he got sold

— subban is the definition of a n*****

— Someone needs to smack PK subban across his big n***** lips. #scumbag

— SUBBAN IS A F****** PORCH M*****

— F*** that stupid m***** #subban

— F*** you subban you f****** lucky ass n**

My goal was to list enough of the tweets thats the reader couldn't help but feel the same thing PK must have felt that night. To no fault of any particular person, the edit came back as follows:

In a series of tweets…

The former forced the reader to feel, the latter allowed the reader to decide if they wanted to absorb the message. Further, we are so conditioned to skimming articles that 'a series of tweets' is simply never clicked on. I didn't like that.

The minute Derek told me I couldn't publish a book without a line edit, it sounded like a challenge. No, I can't publish a book as expected without an edit, but yes I can publish a book no one sees coming, because it's mine.

That said, I don't want an edit. I don't want a big publishing house. I don't want agents or sponsors or anything. I'm sure that in an effort to get this book to you, I will inevitably work with people. I don't produce paper, after all. But to me, all those things, especially working with ghostwriters and the like, produce the type of book you're used to. Line edits regress art to the mean, producing a 'memoir' that feels stiff because even the slightest bit of formula feels formulaic these days.

This is not that.

I've gone through this shit 100x at this point, so if something's off, it's off. I'm not a machine, player. But by doing it this way, I'm allowing you to believe in the authenticity of the words and judge them more wholly. If you love Different Dude, then you know you don't also secretly love a cable company or something. If you hate it, you know it's just some guy with his laptop on his actual lap doing his best.

Now that that's settled, let's get…

GRIMY

My sophomore year of college at Cal started with so much promise. I hadn't played much as a freshman, but in the last few games of the season, I had been given some time and made the most of it. In the 2003 Pac 10 tournament I had seven points and four rebounds in 10 minutes of play. Logically, I thought I could easily average 28 and 16 if the coach gave me 40 minutes. That was dumb as hell.

We had established a pretty tight set of practice rules and understandings in my freshman year as well. The clearest understanding may have been the biggest one: the starters turned their jerseys to the blue side and the bench turned their jerseys to the gold side. I spent the entire time as a freshman wearing a gold jersey, so the hope was that in my second year I could earn my way to the blue team. How else would I make it to the NBA? I'd have to play real minutes at some point.

We had a monster recruiting class that year. I had never seen any of them play, but ask the Rivals.com ratings and they were all top 30 in the country. It was a legit legit recruiting class. My goofy ass did not consider at all, that time does not just move one forward like it had seemed to in high school. Time consistently brings new challenges, and in this case it's name was The Freshman Class.

On the first day of practice, I stood there desperately hoping to make the blue squad.

I had 7 and 4. That was a lot. And it was late in the season. Hell yea I'm a blue guy. The seniors aren't even that good. Bro, we got walk ons ahead of me. It'll be fine.

My internal dialogue was all lies that I fully believed because I was the one peddling them. The coaches read the names of the blue squad. I wasn't one of them.

Fuck. Gold again. This is gonna be a long road to become a starter, but it can be done.

They read the gold team names and I was also not on that list.

WHAT THE FUCK. WHAT THE ACTUAL FUCK?

The shitty part is, I didn't even think about it with that much conviction. It was a sad resignation as I looked at who was left. Myself, a couple walk ons, and David Paris. I wondered if they were just going to kick us out of practice. They didn't seem to need us, so what was the point? Nothing is worse than watching other people practice while you stand there thinking it could be you. That's when they brought out these red thin mesh overlay jerseys and handed them to the rest of us.

"You guys will be Gold-B for now."

FOR NOW MY ASS.

"Yes, coach."

I let my head sink into my shoulders. This was a common response from me at the time. It was clear that there were winners and losers and I would be one of the losers. In an instant, I could map out my entire future as some dude who works at AT&T. No shade to anyone who works there, but I just imagined every day some yokel asking me why I was there and not in the NBA. The answer would be simple: because I wasn't good enough.

"These some grimy ass jerseys," David let out. I guess at least I wasn't alone.

That night, I went home and called my mom. It was time to transfer. This was no easy task back then, given that I'd have to leave the conference and sit a year and lose a year. But fuck it, what other choice did I have? For me, I've never been someone to give up, but have also always looked for a short cut. In that moment, my mom recognized my exit strategy right away.

"No."

"No? I'm saying I'm gonna come to San Diego State. I'll be close to home, I'll play, and I can be close to [my great grandmother]."

"No. You chose Berkeley, stay at Berkeley."

I was confused that my mom didn't want me to come home. She sure seemed to lament my not being there. Maybe that was just general mom speak and she was actually super happy to have me gone. Or maybe there was something else. Either way, at that age it felt like I couldn't leave without her support, so I decided to stay.

When I woke up the next day, I had hella resolve. If I was going to stay, something had to change. Nothing for me would improve if I just showed up and followed the script. I had had a similar situation in high school, but with less stakes, so I channeled my AAU coach, Jeff, who helped me navigate these things. He hated the system that my high school promoted and also used to tell me to go back there and hurt people. Seriously. Not in a weird way, but he would say things like "take the ball and throw it right at the coach's face. Kick Ryan in the balls man. Fuck those people."

In his own way, he had given me a lesson and although I never hit anyone, it had kind of worked in high school.

So here I was confronted with another situation that felt the same, but was very different. It was going to take more than a kick to the balls to change my whole life. I was going to have to slap the shit out of someone.

When I left the apartment that day, I left with a very specific task: I was going to slap the shit out of the first teammate I saw that day. It was obviously a shitty plan for many reasons, but it was all I had. More aggression would be the key. I would just wait until I saw someone on our team then slap 'em on sight. Simples.

But it was not quite as simple as that. I didn't see anyone the whole day, which was unusual. I was hoping to knock this out (pun intended) before lunch so we could all calm down before practice. That didn't happen.

We got all the way to practice time and still nothing. So I went to the locker room and prepared to do this the hard way. I punched in the code and when I opened the door, there were six or seven dudes in there already, one with his back to me a couple feet away. No one was paying attention. Why would they?

I tapped that teammate whose back was to me on the shoulder and, before he could fully get his head around, I slapped THE SHIT out of him. I had recently seen Chappelle's Show and I think I channeled that aggression unnecessarily. The point was the slap, not to fuck him up. I may as well have asked him what the five fingers said to the face. It was actually crazy.

He took the hit and stood there shocked for three to four seconds. Everyone did, myself included. I could see everyone registering what had just happened in real time.

Someone just got slapped!

Chris got slapped!

Rod slapped Chris?!

Rod, the corny nigga from Cardiff By The Sea, San Diego, slapped Chris?!

Once the fourth question had an answer, Chris beat me up. I mean, everyone stopped him but if they hadn't, who knows? He was my size essentially, this wasn't just some dude. I was still like 190 lbs and I didn't just learn how to fight well overnight.

I kinda just let it happen. I don't even remember feeling anything. I was numb. I had no plan for what would come after the slap. This was supposed to happen at lunch.

What came next was interesting. We went to practice and everyone was not only upset, but it was all they could talk about. It was, after all, probably the only time in any of our lives we would ever see some shit like that. What I couldn't predict was that there was a slight hitch people started to develop around me. I had broken social contract, so now I was like a homeless person on the street to them. Maybe even a rabid dog. I was liable to bite at a moment's notice. That scared people. I was someone who could act in any way at any time for any reason. It was a weirdly powerful feeling. I ran with it.

New things began to happen in practice going forward: the first was that I started being a dick at all times. I wrote the word GRIMY on my shoes in big letters every time I didn't play in the game. I started screaming at everyone. Pushing them. Hitting them. It was mean.

The other thing, though, was that I got way better at basketball right away. Like lightning fast.

I remember one day, I stole the ball from someone, took it coast to coast, dunked it, took the ball out of the net so no one could take it out, punted it into the stands, turned to the coaches and screamed "GIVE ME SOME FUCKING MINUTES!"

I was kicked out of the gym.

GOOD. FUCK 'EM.

But, shit, talent is talent and mine was starting to show. No one could do shit about it. I was just getting better and better so I kept getting more time in practice. This whole shit upset a lot of guys.

One day, after training-table (post practice meal), I was walking out holding my food in a to-go box. A teammate of mine, fed up with the last few weeks in general and an elbow specifically levied that day, walked up and knocked the food out of my hand and it fell and hit the floor. He looked up at me (he was a PG), and instinctively, I put both my hands around his neck and pressed him into the wall of the hallway.

"Are you calm? Are you calm? Are you calm?" I kept asking him.

"Yea…" he said as best he could. I was cutting off a little air, so I backed off and left.

THE WAY THIS STORY SPREAD HOLY SHIT. Let some of the guys tell it and I had him by one arm with his feet dangling inches off the ground. It was the ultimate punking. Like the final retaliation after years of being told I was too soft.

Softness is fucking made up. The skinniest dude here has y'all shook.

After that day, I was never bad at basketball again. Being unpredictable made people just as scared as any amount of strength did.

The next season I was on the blue team because I was becoming that dude and for no other reason. I went on to be named (I guess it was unofficial) the most improved player in the country after averaging less than a point in my first two years and leading the team in scoring and rebounding in my third.

Rewriting this now, something is clear that I never realized before. It was never about how strong or weak I was, it was about smaller people making me feel small. Once I stood fully in my truth, they couldn't hold me. And it wasn't just on the court that took off either. Off it, I made better friendships, finally started getting female attention, and I became the life of the party.

It was like life had one big on/off switch and I finally switched mine on.

ALL OF THE LIGHTS

When I announced I was retiring, everyone thought it was premature. I did not. I was done with the game. I was done with Korea. I was ready to start building my relationship with Sharon. I was ready to become a regular guy.

During the last game of the season, game six of a seven game series, I sat there before the game going through my usual pregame routine. As I was wrapping up my meditation (I'd do it two minutes before the Korean National Anthem), I opened my eyes and finally saw what I should have really seen years before.

There were lights everywhere. All the fans had light up sticks waving side to side in unison, there were dozens of drones with lights on them circling overhead, beaming lasers everywhere. The cheerleaders were holding sparklers and, to top it all off, there was a video presentation on a piece of fabric that stretched from the roof to the floor. It was so fucking cool.

I had been in Korea for a decade. I had seen these images a thousand times. Only on this very last time did it connect for me just how beautiful the entire experience was. My mind raced through my career as if it were my life flashing before my eyes. Tears welled up as the drones swirled overhead. It was really over.

As I returned to the present, I felt overwhelmed and proud. I had really played pro basketball for 12 years. It was crazy to think about. I hadn't just done it. I had crushed it. And in that moment I felt all of that positive energy swirling around me as I let my career go into the night. We lost by one, and that was it.

That was the first time I retired.

WHITE GIRL LIKE KOBE

I was 13 when my mom told my brother and me to jump in the minivan. We were going up to LA to visit my grandmother at her job. I didn't question why we were going, but it did seem that we often went to visit family members at work.

When we got there, my grandmother seemed excited to see me. This never happened before then. In fact, she was often unkind to me at best. For example, against my wishes, she never allowed me to keep toys or video games at her house. So, yea, it was weird that she ran up and hugged me.

"How tall are you now?" she asked. "You're so handsome!"

"6'1" I think."

"I have to show you off!"

No one told me why we were walking in, but I was just taken into an office park with the family. Granny walked me through some random company while each of her 'friends' (coworkers) inspected me and commented on my height. It was super awkward for me and only me. Everyone else delighted in who I was and what my basketball future would be. They grabbed my arms to measure and took pictures with me, back to back. I wasn't even on a team.

After the parade was over, my grandmother walked me out to the car, alone.

"Now that you're tall and handsome, you're going to go right to the NBA. Don't forget about us," she said.

I didn't really even know her, save for terrible things.

"I would never forget about you," I lied.

She looked up at me and the sun was in her eyes.

"Don't marry no white girl like Kobe."

REPRESENT YOUR HOOD

I was waiting in the lobby of the Beijing Ritz-Carlton until TJ Ford got down. There was a full day off the next day, so I asked him if there was anything to do. Not only did I not know shit about Beijing, I also hoped that the superstars in the room knew something I didn't. I was right. TJ told me to meet him in the lobby, so I waited.

Carmelo, JR, and Renaldo Balkman walked by and out the front door. I watched as a swarm of Chinese suits guided them into a limo.

Dope

TJ finally made his way down with a couple other guys, maybe Danny Granger. He looked at me and pointed to the limo. I guess we were also getting in.

SUPER DOPE.

We got into the limo, which instantly felt too small for 10 seven footers, and I was seated directly across from NBA legends I had never really met. I say 'really' because I had met Carmelo in high school. It was during a 55 point loss to Baltimore Select at the Adidas Big Time in Las Vegas. He had 40 with a head full of rainbow berets. I had 7 with a tidy haircut. I digress. I didn't believe I was actually in the room. I felt like a highly privileged fly on the wall more than one of the guys. I listened.

We pulled into some club. There was Jordan branding everywhere, a red carpet, and all kinds of shit I really didn't see coming when I was told to come downstairs. It was a Carmelo branded event and he was the guest of honor.

That makes sense.

We sat at a booth while Melo did his thing. My seat, thank God, was right next to two gorgeous Australian models. I didn't even consider that international models would be in Beijing. That lack of consideration didn't matter. We were now fully chopping it up. I was no longer a fly on the wall, I was an NBA dude at a party. I was living it.

I had no experience talking to international models, so when they showed genuine interest in me (or the experience, does it matter?) I lost my fucking shit. I was in love with both of them. Equally and fully. I started planning trips to Melbourne (ahem, Mel-bine) and everything. That was when Taraji P Henson walked in.

Taraji has a gravity to her. It's like we all started leaning her direction and it wasn't even sexual. Some people just got the juice.

She explained that she was in town to shoot The Karate Kid with Jaden Smith and Jackie Chan. I was fully mind blown as she was explaining that she was learning Mandarin and all this shit. I had to take stock of the situation: I was on the Pacers, sitting at a table with NBA All Stars, Tara P Henson was practicing Chinese, Carmelo was signing autographs for fans in the background, and on either side of me were two of the most beautiful women I had ever met.

WHAT ACTUALLY IS LIFE?

"You wanna meet Jackie?"

Taraji snapped me out of my daydream.

I thought she was talking to me, but clearly she was talking to Melo who was back at the table. I was not in control here whatsoever. Melo kinda shrugged yes and we started to get ready to leave. I wish I had footage of this moment as I got up with this group of legends and hot people, and walked outside AS A UNIT.

This move would require us to pack into taxis. The limo was gone and not coming back until the event was over, but we were calling an audible at Taraji's direction. She directed everything, including the seating arrangements for the taxis. She then spoke fucking Mandarin to all the drivers to give them directions and jumped in the lead taxi. Baller shit.

I got into the middle taxi of the three, and my two Australian boo-thangs got into the third. We couldn't all fit. It was fine, though, because we weren't going too far. I looked up to the lead taxi and could see Taraji signal. We started rolling. At the first light, we made a right and the taxi behind me went left.

Did their driver know a shortcut?

We pulled up to a different Ritz-Carlton which I thought was weird, and I immediately looked for the other taxi. It was nowhere to be found. Taraji was laughing.

"Fuck those bitches!"

She had told their driver to go somewhere else. Now thinking about it, I have no idea where she sent them and I hope they're ok. I wanted to be upset, but that Taraji energy, man. It felt like I should just trust the process a little bit, you know?

We walked into the RC and got into an elevator. I, Taraji, Melo, TJ, JR, Blakman, Danny, and I want to say Josh McRoberts all piled in. Taraji hit B13. It hit me that the hotel had 40 floors above ground and 13 below. I can't lie, I didn't trust Beijing enough to trust what would happen 150 feet below ground, but down we went.

When we got to the bottom, ahead of us was a long hallway lined with red wallpaper. The room opened up to the right at the end of the hall and I could see flashing lights coming around the corner and bouncing off the wall of the hallway. I could also hear what sounded like wailing. Not screaming, but like a wailing sound that seemed to have a point.

We exited the elevator and as I walked down that hallway, the lights got brighter and the whaling transitioned and started to sound like singing. When I turned the corner, there was Jackie Chan surrounded by 20 Chinese women singing Karaoke at the top of his lungs. He saw us and jumped up.

"Ta ra ji!"

This was stimulation overload. Everything I looked at was either new, weird, or cool as fuck. EVERYTHING. The walls were cool and textured. The women were almost like decor because they moved and didn't speak much. Like performance art. The cigars Jackie pulled out smelled like success in television and film. He told us stories that were each more interesting than the last.

Jackie eventually asked me why I didn't have a cigar in my hand. The truth was twofold: I didn't know how to smoke one and I was deathly afraid of nicotine.

"I'm just chillin right now," was what I said out loud.

I'll never forget what he said in reply.

"I'll teach you. I represent my hood. Chris Tucker taught me to represent my hood."

THIS IS THE SINGLE GREATEST MOMENT OF MY LIFE

This man then took me step by step through the process of smoking a cigar while everyone drank and smoked on the 13th floor down. Y'all can't tell me shit.

DRUG WARS

In the summer of 2001, I started playing AAU basketball and most of the games were in LA. On this particular occasion it was a pretty standard trip, meaning we played two days of games at either Cal-State Dominguez Hills or at Lynwood HS. Honestly, 95% of games I played in AAU were at one of those two locations for whatever reason.

Regardless of the reason, we usually piled into whatever the cheapest hotel was in the area, and this trip was no exception. We shacked up at a Motel 6 situation roadside near Lynwood high and called it a night. I'm unsure how we even afforded that.

On the first day of this trip, during a game, I injured something on my body that I really can't remember, but it prevented me from going to get dinner with the team. There was a Carl's Jr nearby and they had all gone, but I didn't go because I was being pouty about my injury. I wasn't a hardened athlete yet by any means, so I needed everyone to know not only that I was injured, but that it hurt, and that's why I was playing badly.

But when the team got back with those coddamn burgers, I couldn't help it. The hunger was stronger than my bullshit injury. I was still trying to act like it was painful, but it was actually fine by that point. I was not going to miss out on a Famous Star. Not today, Satan. I headed to the Carl's Jr around the block, alone.

On the 100 yard walk back to the telly, 3 dudes jumped out of a bush in front of me and started walking the same direction. I knew this movie. I slowed down and so did they. I definitely knew this movie. They then turned around and one of them trained a gun on me.

"The backpack," one of them said quickly.

Oh snap.

I had forgotten I brought my backpack with me.

Why bring my backpack on a 100 yard walk, you ask? Because I had lazily grabbed it due to the fact that it had my TI-83+ graphing calculator inside and, this is true, I was programming my own version of "Drug Wars" that used names and scenarios directly related to my high school. Any time I wasn't playing, I was programming. I didn't even program on this short walk, though. It was just a habit to grab the bag by then.

I started to hand them my backpack, through tears. Then something came over me.

"Can I get my calculator please?"

"What?" The guy with the gun did the talking and he sounded confused.

"I'm sorry I really need it for school."

"Hold on," he said and turned to his boys.

No joke, they sat there and debated for like 10 seconds. I actually assumed they were just going to surprise shoot me, so I was ready for anything. Maybe I could run away, but as many movies have taught me, outrunning bullets is a fool's errand.

My thoughts were interrupted when they started digging through the backpack to give my Texas Instrument back to me. I thought it was a joke, but they kept rummaging. They couldn't find the calculator. I then asked if I could look. For some reason, they let me take my bag back and go through it. After a few seconds, I realized it wasn't there! I forgot I had taken it out earlier and didn't put it back in the bag.

WHOOOOOOOOOOOOOOOOOOOPS

In a panic, I pretended to have grabbed the TI-83+ and returned the backpack to them. They ran off into the night, and that was that.

When I got back to the room, everyone could see I now had no backpack and I was crying. At first, they joked about my injury, but very soon they could tell it was real. I told them what had happened, and they actually really all had my back. I never mentioned the calculator part though. I felt like they wouldn't have wanted me to be their teammate anymore if I did and I couldn't have that. I needed them. Even at that moment, all I wanted was to not look like a bitch.

PLAYER.

How tall are you? Tall? Super tall? Mega tall?

If you're tall enough, you should definitely play basketball -- I know I would if I was your height!

it's the best! If you're broke and wanna buy your momma a house, this is for you!

If you and the homies got no hoes, grab a ball and start dribbling! You could be paid and laid soon, all you need to do is give up every single thing that makes you human! But don't take our word for it -- Ask your local pro today!

ADVICE

In my first week as a college basketball player, an upperclassmen teammate gave me a ride home to my dorm. On the way, we chatted about college life and its trappings. Eventually I asked him what was the one piece of advice I should take with me for the next four years.

"Always flush the condoms," he said intensely. "Hoes be poking holes in that shit."

He then asked if there were hot freshmen in the dorms I could hook him up with.

MINICAMPS

I'm sure most people reading this have no idea what a mini-camp is. To be honest, I didn't really know until I attended one. The name is pretty accurate. Whereas the entire franchise participates in normal NBA training camps and they lasts a month, a mini-camp usually lasts a few days and has few players. If there was something close to a try-out, a mini-camp would be it.

My first mini-camp was with the Golden State Warriors. It was fitting, seeing as I was local and I'm sure they just needed a third body. I don't remember who the second guy was, but I do remember that Marco Killingsworth was the guy they were actually looking at. He was an All-American from Indiana who was known for playing very beast-like. He definitely lived up to his reputation.

I had never even played a real game as a professional and it showed. In the first drill, both of the other guys backed me right down and scored. The coach stopped practice for a minute.

"You haven't done this yet have you?"

He was smiling so I didn't take offense.

"What? Yes. No? What?"

"You're playing defense like a college kid. You just let them get right into your body and back you down. In the NBA you can do this. And this."

He was motioning an arm bar and an off hand. I mimicked his motion and he nodded. When the drill resumed, my defense was instantly much much better. It was time for the next drill.

This time I had to line up on one block while Killingsworth lined up on the other. The coach threw him the ball and I was supposed to meet him at the rim and attempt to block him. On the first attempt he dunked it before I could even jump. I looked back at the coach thinking there was some other secret. There wasn't. This was going to be when the men separated themselves from the boys, and they did.

Marco proceeded to dunk on me like 15 times. I was not invited to Summer League.

NEW SMELLS

I've only ever been "scouted" from the stands by a woman twice. By that, I mean that there was someone watching me play while simultaneously sending me a romantic DM. Both times were unexpected.

The first time, I was in France. I was very busy not playing, as per usual, when I looked up behind the north basket. I saw a bad Moroccan woman staring me right in the eye. I looked left and back at her. She shook her head. I looked right and again she shook her head. I then pointed at myself and mouthed the word "me?' She nodded.

Afterwards, there was a DM awaiting me on MySpace. I couldn't believe that it actually worked that way. She asked me out, and out we went. It was fun for a while, especially the kind of weird excitement accompanying the circumstances of our connection.

In the end, between the language barrier and the new smells, it didn't last long.

ORGANIC MATERIAL

It's weird to remember how awkward certain things about college were. One of those things for me was the fact that despite Berkeley being a college town, without a car you were basically fucked. The city is built on a hill and that hill was incredibly taxing to walk up and down, especially after practice. So when I had the chance to get my mom's 1996 Nissan Quest minivan, I jumped at the opportunity.

Fast forward to November 22nd, 2005. Yes, I remember the exact day because it's the day that XBOX 360 dropped. That's right, this is an XBOX related story. This was actually the second release date of that year. The first one, before Halloween, saw lines upwards of 200 people at the Emeryville Best Buy. So when I drove past that same Best Buy on November 22nd expecting to get some info and saw there was already a line forming, I did something impulsive: I got out of the car and got in line. I then called my teammate to come bring me some blankets and shit and I spent the night outside of the Best Buy, mid season.

I didn't anticipate the rain that came and soaked me and all my blankets, but I pushed through. At 8 a.m., the doors opened, and I sprinted into the store to grab my 360. My teammate then circled back to pick me up and I went back to my apartment.

The issue was that we were supposed to travel to the University of Oregon the next day for a game and I was exhausted, so I forgot to get the wet blankets out of the van before I left town. Big mistake. Huge.

When I got back to Berkeley and opened the car, it was bad. It smelled like mildew and ass (everything smelled like ass until I was like 23), and mold had already overtaken the blankets. This had quickly become a problem I didn't have the time or energy to solve, because we had fully started the Pac 10 schedule. I needed to get a detail, but I didn't have detail money. It was at this moment I made a pivotal choice. I asked Donovan to help me clean the whip in exchange for $50.

Donovan was homeless as far as I, or anyone, knew. He was close to our age, maybe 25 tops, looked a bit rough, but not necessarily like someone living on the streets. Word around town was that he audited classes at Berkeley and was planning to start his own auto shop. I knew him because this woman I was interested in knew him. That's how simple the times were back in 2005. He gladly accepted my offer to clean the car and I left town again for another road trip.

Hey bro where's your car?

I should have taken this text from my friend back in Berkeley as a sign, but I did not. Instead I replied with the truth:

Donovan took it to clean, don't trip.

DONOVAN!?

I should have taken the all caps "DONOVAN" as a sign, but I did not. Instead I replied with the truth:

Yes.

When we got back into town, the car was not back. I wanted to panic a little bit, but again, now we were fully into my senior season. I was dealing with injuries and scouts and my first GF, Maria, and a lot of things. When the car was missing, I played it down to folks to save face, but really it was a WTF moment.

I realized that I never once considered that Donovan didn't have a cell phone. Every time I had ever spoken to him, it was because we ran into one another on the streets. So with my car gone and no way to contact him, I went on about my life, or so I tried. Every single person I knew was aware of the situation and would text me from their T-Mobile Sidekicks with reports of the Quest's location.

> Yo! Your whip is at the Ralphs! Get down here!

> I seen the Quest parked hella far down
> Telegraph. Is that you?

It was not me. This went on for weeks.

One day, about a month after he first took it, I came home and the car was in the garage. A miracle! I ran down and unlocked the gate. I opened the car and... whoa. Every inch of the car had something in it. It wasn't garbage, but it also wasn't usable goods. It was just filled with... things. Flies buzzed around. THE WET BLANKETS WERE STILL SITTING THERE. I felt so defeated that I just locked the car and went upstairs. Sure enough, the next morning the car was gone again.

This was when the reports started to change.

> Yo that man DONOVAN is definitely LIVING in
> your whip!

> Bro no way I seen this dude eating a burrito in
> your shit in East Oakland.

Embarrassed, I kept pretending it was part of the plan. It was not. I don't think I saw my moms minivan for months. It kinda just belonged to him now. As graduation approached, I knew I would have to tell my mom that I had made a tax deductible donation to the streets. As I planned what I would say, I got a call from her.

"Where's my car?"

I almost wanted to hit her with a "where's your car dude?" but I refrained. Instead I lied.

"I'm about to drive it right now!"

"No. You're not," she said sternly. She knew something I didn't.

The car had been impounded a week earlier and because it was her car, they sent the notice to her in San Diego. I had to explain the entire situation to her, which was brutal enough. What was more brutal was her "well, figure it out" mentality in response. To this day, I'm unsure if it ever fully registered to her that I had given *her* car to a strange homeless man. Whatever. I made my bed and now I'd have to drive in it.

Since the notice was over a week old, the bill sat at like $600 and was growing. Every day I took to get the whip out would be another $75 I absolutely didn't have. The quickest, and most ironic, way to get cash fast was to sell the XBOX 360 and the games. I'll never forget, I met some dude at the BART station in downtown Berkeley and traded him $600 for EVERYTHING. Guys, I was a top 500 Madden player with no system or game. This yokel took everything.

I then went directly to the impound with a notarized letter from my mom authorizing me to get the car. When I handed it to the dude working the impound, who I'm sure has seen some shit in his day, he looked right at me and laughed. Hard.

I should have taken the laughter as a sign, but I did not. Instead I replied with laughter of my own.

"Haaaa! Yeaa…"

He pointed out the van, still laughing, and left me to it. When I opened the driver side door, trash fell out. Not 'things.' Trash. A lot of it. The smell nearly laid me out. It was a giant green dumpster. I looked back at the guy who was doubled over laughing.

And that man has seen some shit.

I got in and sat on top of all sorts of organic material.

I just gotta get the car home.

I started the engine and it made a weird empty wailing sound. I looked at the guy again, his face had gone from brown to red with laughter. You'd think he'd seen some shit before, but this really sent him. I guess Donovan had made some 'upgrades' to the engine?

I hit the gas and the car gave a squeal and started moving. For like nine feet. Then it ran out of gas. I looked back. You'd think this man was being tickled by God himself. His eyes were damn near falling out of his skull, and he was coughing now because no man can laugh that hard for that long with dying apparently.

I then had to get out and pay the laughing man $5 for gas, which he siphoned out of an RV. It was all random and way too hot for all this on a 100 degree day in San Leandro.

With the siphoned gas in the whip, I drove home and started cleaning. I cleaned that bitch for eight consecutive hours. I couldn't do shit about the sound of the engine, but I made it look and smell decent.

I then listed it for sale and a man and his family came to look at it that same night. He wanted to give it the once over, which I was nervous about, but when he got in he said it smelled nice.

OKAYYY.

He then started the engine and it squealed like before. I looked at him. He turned to me and paused for a second to hear more clearly.

"This has an upgraded muffler, doesn't it?" He asked.

WHAT? YOU IDIOT? OMG WHAT?

"Actually it did have some engine work," I replied in absolute truth. "A friend did it for me."

He bought it from me on the spot. I took the cash and sent most of it to my mom so she could start a new life without me. I spent the rest on a new Xbox 360. I was reduced to just Madden and no other games, but we were back. It would be four years before I owned a vehicle again..

So in the end, I learned a few very valuable lessons

1. Cleaning your own car ain't that hard, genius
2. Maybe don't give your keys to someone without a phone
3. If I hadn't been so embarrassed, any one of my friends could have gotten the car back for me
4. Don't fall for muffler upgrades no matter how cool the engine sounds

IT'S ALL BULLSHIT

My first season in Korea had a lot of question marks. The Korean coaches were generally creatures of habit, so a whole new type of player like me was a risk. Many thought I might not do well. My team was projected to finish 6th out of ten teams, and the media gave coach Kang Dong Hee a lot of shit for going with me, especially once I showed up to the draft in all neon. But this man had vision.

That's not to say he wasn't testing me, though. We would scrimmage Korean college teams in the preseason. Some games we would win by 60, some we would win by seven. That's just hoops. It was not just hoops to Kang, though. The close games were followed by conditioning the second the game was over.

In one of these scrimmages, my teammates were playing like garbage. The score was closer than I liked, so I took over. I might have scored around 50 points in a close win. Kang was not satisfied.

"He says you have to do conditioning," the translator, Tei, announced.

"Why? I'm tired as fuck, man. It's not my fault the game was close."

"That's a good point but…" Tei loved to trail off instead of deliver bad news.

A few seconds later, we lined up to do our most intense conditioning drill. It was kind of a modified 3 man weave, but one where I would have to both take the ball out and make the layup on each side, 10 times in a row. It sucked.

I had the spirit of the game in me, though. I was so fucking angry that I had to do the bullshit conditioning that I got an adrenaline boost. Not only did I complete the drill with relative ease, I dunked each one. On the last one, I took the ball out of the net and threw it.

"WHAT THE FUCK IS THIS?!" I screamed as the ball bounced around the stands.

Tei SPRINTED over to me.

"Why did you do this? Why did you throw the ball?!"

Kang was yelling and pointing at the door. He wanted me to leave.

Tei continued, "He says you have to go. I'm sorry you have to go away!"

I walked outside and Tei directed me to the team bus to cool off. Tensions were high. He was sure I was going to be kicked out of the league. But when the head coach came, he basically said he liked that fire. Still, he made it clear that I had to channel that same aggression on the court or they were going to get someone to replace me real quick. Put up or shut up, for all intents and purposes.

We won the first real game of the season by 30. But! The team we beat was projected to be in last place, something Tei made sure I knew afterwards.

"Coach is very happy with your condition today. But he is worried about Leather."

"Leather?"

"Terrance Leather. He's the best. MVP player."

"What team is he on?" I had a feeling I knew the answer.

"SK. Next game. I don't want to put pressure but we must win, ok? Please win."

"Ok man, relax," I said both fully understanding and having no clue about the stakes.

Enter Terrence Leather. Leather was indeed the man in Korea. Every country has a "the guy" and he was him. He led the league in scoring for years, rebounded like an actual mad man, and he had this jerky way about him. He could get to his spots almost as if defenders weren't trying to stop him. There was no doubt he was good. The film didn't lie.

He was also rough around the edges. Maybe intentionally? I'll never know for sure. But Imagine if KD let his hair grow out a bit. Like just enough to where people would ask him if he intended to take it all the way to a fro. The nappy and wild nature of Leather's hair looked like that. His actual face was menacing. I think this added to Leather's game. He didn't *look* nice. He sure as hell didn't play nice either.

When the SK game came about, all eyes were on me. People had taken notice of what I could do, but to be the best you gotta beat the best, and no matter what league you're in around the world, folks wanna know if you're the best. Shit, I wanted to know if I was the best. There's nothing like weeks of people telling you about some dude you never heard of as if he's daddy Jesus or something. It can be quite motivating. They all knew what they were doing.

I don't remember exactly how it went, but we absolutely beat the brakes off of SK. Man alive, it was brutal. I almost felt bad for them, especially Leather, the same way I almost feel bad for Thanos when he's finally losing in Endgame. I think we STARTED the game on a 24-0 run. When one of their guys finally scored, our fans cheered out of pity. Damn that shit was epic.

Not only had leather finished with his season low, we had won by 25 and I had done considerable work. After the game, Kang gave me a look as if to say "nigga literally punt the ball to the moon if you want as long as you keep playing like this." Yea, his look included the good version of the N-word somehow.

Leather and I battled for the next two years, and it was always brutal. I didn't always get the best of him either. Like I said, he's very good at basketball and was the reigning MVP. We would talk hella trash to one another too. We wouldn't smile at each other at the club (which I consider a true sign of hatred). We would do petty shit on and off the court.

It came to a head for me in the 2012 playoffs. I went up for a layup and he elbowed me in the face. I was down for a minute and everyone was going crazy. They reviewed it and whatnot. I don't remember which way the call went, but I thought I had never been more flagrantly violated in my whole career. Two minutes later I was fine and we swept them in the end anyways but, after that, I decided that I hated Terrence Leather for life.

At the beginning of the next year, we had media day a couple days before the start of the season. Normally American players aren't invited to do that, but this year we were. I knew I'd have to see ol' Leatherface himself. I wasn't happy about it. So when I showed up and saw him, I damn near snarled. I hated even seeing him in the wild.

Unexpectedly, he walked right up to me without hesitation, the first time we had been face to face since the elbow.

"Benson," he started as I clinched my fist, "you know I fuck with you, right?"

I let my fist go.

"What?"

"Benson. We are both black. I like you. This is all bullshit. All this shit is bullshit. You and me the only black niggas here."

I looked around the room. That wasn't entirely accurate, but I understood his point. In a country with 50 Million Koreans, there were only 20 of us. We were all we had. Why would we take it so far as to hate one another?

After that, I never hated an opponent again.

I DON'T LIKE PEOPLE PLAYING ON MY PHONE

I was fast asleep when my phone rang. I turned it to silent without thinking and went back to bed. Again it rang, and the dull buzz of a phone in 2008 was enough to annoy me out of bed.

"What!?" I screamed at my phone in the darkness.

It was Madison, my girlfriend at the time.

"Turn on the news. Obama won!"

I checked the clock. It was close to 3am.

Oh shit. It is election night.

I had nearly forgotten because I was in France and didn't head out to the polls as I was accustomed to back home.

I rushed to the living room and turned on the TV. I thought I might have to search a while to find the coverage. I was wrong. Every damn channel in France was broadcasting Obama's acceptance speech. I sat there in the middle of the night alone and watched for an hour, crying.

WAGS.

Congrats! You did it! You got you a man who scores baskets for a living.

There have only ever been 5000 people to play in the league, and you gonna have his babies!

It's giving push the Ghost down Sunset energy with a bit of Media Take Out. It's everything you ever wanted.

It's ok that he's never around! What even is Christmas? You never cared about your birthday. This is what Facetime is for!

Build your brand, because the future is uncertain and the hype is right now!

DD
DIFFERENT DUDE™

EWW

My best friend Alex went to see Love and Basketball in theaters when it came out. I asked him how it was.

"Too much love, not enough basketball," he sighed.

"Eww."

BOOMTHO

adv. 1: An occurrence of an uncommonly good thing.

2. An exclamation or show of excitement.

boom got them tho!

verb. 1a: The self completion of an uncommonly good thing.

1b: The successful act of mating.

boom got them dos!

verb. 1: The exact double of boom got them tho!

2: The completion of a difficult shot attempt on the basketball court.

Speaker 1: I just won the lotto

Speaker 2: Boom tho!

Going into the fall of 2006, I was broke-broke-broke. I say it three times because I've been broke many times, including right now, but in those cases there was always something I had been working and saving for. In 2006, I was just broke because I was waiting around for a basketball season to start that would hardly pay me even when I signed. This was real broke-ness.

As season approached, I left Sacramento and headed to San Francisco to stay with JGant to not feel so helpless. JGant's mom made food every day (a lot of it), the house was clean and nice, and most of all, they allowed me to stay indefinitely. Looking back, I'm sure Mr and Mrs Gant took one look at a young brotha and knew damn well that I was in need of shelter and materials.

It was at this time that JGant and I were at our wildest. We were just weird, man. JGant, Ramy, Clay, Elram, and I would walk around the streets of The City spouting absolute gibberish. Legitimate gibberish.

"Hey scrape up boop got eeeem!"

"In there like swimwear thooooo!"

"Ready like spaghetti tho boop!"

Once again, this was complete nonsense. Said in the right environment, however, these words would get folks hyped up. There would exist a normal San Francisco or Berkeley party, brimming with relatively boring white folks, and then we would walk in sounding like an intentionally scratchy E-40 record and turn that bitch upside down.

Honestly, it was so wholesome, too. We weren't druggies. We didn't fight people or buy bottles (couldn't afford them). We hardly even hit on any women. We just danced and celebrated so damn hard that people couldn't deny whatever we were doing.

Around Halloween, I got the idea to make a music video. Well, I got the idea to make *another* music video because I had already made one. In my Senior year, around Valentines Day, my teammate and I made a HORRIBLE music video for our then girlfriends that got like 2000 views in a few hours before I shut it down. I was shook at the time.

How the hell did people I didn't send it to even see it? Why would they want to? I made it for her! All of these ideas were new and confusing. I figured I'd see if I could intentionally make something that I had control over and see if people would watch as well.

I'm unsure how I did it, but I convinced JGant to rap and we made a song. We used the mic on the white MacBook my agent had bought me to record and GarageBand to "mix," whatever that meant. My bars were not good and difficult to get through. It was really just a struggle getting the volume right using a tiny hole built into my computer. That said, JGant was worse. Way way worse. Man's couldn't keep a beat at all. Couldn't write a bar at all. Couldn't even conceptualize the process. It was both funny and maddening.

I had to write both our parts and spend hella time editing his parts so they could sound somewhat on beat. I did my best to combine all the phrases we had been saying in a way that could be repeatable. The hook ended up working in unexpected ways:

She's ready like spaghetti

We're in there like swimwear

You already know

Boom got them tho

With the rise of Mike Jones, Ying Yang Twins, etc, the simple hooks were hella catchy and mine fit the bill. It's still so catchy that I'm now singing it as I type. I'm unsure how we tapped into that, but we did.

We then walked the MacBook around San Francisco on Halloween attempting to get people to say "boom go them tho" on camera. I was dressed as Flavor Flav, JGant was Mr T, and we walked around bombarding people, asking them to say a phrase they never heard before.

To my surprise, people loved that shit. I couldn't believe how easy it was to get people to just say some dumb shit for no reason, on camera. It wasn't even a real camera. We didn't own anything resembling a real camera. This was a 15 inch white MacBook, flipped open, with Photo Booth on, recording video. Shit must have about 48 total pixels. It was a dumb move, walking my computer around to various Halloween parties, shrouded in drunk 23 year olds, but we did it.

When I finally cut the video together and dropped it, we thought it was the funniest shit that mankind had ever seen. It was obviously quite crude, both because of the tools used to create it and because the man behind the tools was not at all versed in the technique. Still, it was a fucking masterpiece to us. I put it out hoping to get the same people who laughed at my Valentines Day video to see me as a cool guy who can make cool shit.

I'm unsure the video succeeded in changing perceptions, but the formula definitely proved effective. When I woke up the next day, "BOOM GOT THEM THO" had over 20,000 views. I couldn't believe any of it.

Why do random people want to watch us do random shit? It doesn't make sense.

By the end of the day, the video had approached 40,000 views. In 2006 terms, it may as well have been a billion. No one really knew what to do next, so we just let it rock until I went into my season. I was drafted by the Austin Toros a week later and I was off to begin my pro career in the D-League.

The video lived on youtube and was embedded on my new website, toomuchrodbenson.com. TMRB began as a home for dumb recaps of things nobody cared about. The only popular section, which grew exponentially in size after BGTT, was "Funny Myspace Messages." I'd just copy and paste funny myspace messages from people I felt had funny profiles or awful pickup lines. Between the video and the myspace messages, the site started to get some traction.

By the spring, Draft Express hit me up and asked if I'd be willing to write the same stuff there. At like $65 a blog it would double my D-League salary, so I agreed. I began writing and producing the same content on TMRB and DE simultaneously, expanding my reach into spaces where only the nerdiest basketball fans lived. And there we coalesced. Many of them were kids, in middle or high school, and now some of them work at ESPN. Funny how time works.

BOOMTHO went to another level when Sports Illustrated put out a blog ranking all the athlete bloggers on earth and they ranked me #1. I used to say that's because I was the only one doing it, and that's true, but I give myself more credit now. No one was doing it because they hadn't thought to do it. Sometimes you have to acknowledge that the thing was special just because you did it, you know?

After that, BGTT got another 10k views in a day. The same day, which was my birthday, Lawrence Frank (begrudgingly, it seemed) had to acknowledge my #1 rating in front of the team. The Nets all applauded me even though I was bad at basketball and they hardly knew me.

Yahoo! called the next day and asked me to sign with them. The call that changed everything, though, came from PONY Shoes. One of their creative leads, Colin Brickley, had gotten wind of the BOOMTHO movement and decided I'd be a prime candidate for my own shoe.

NIGGA WE MADE IT

I was taken down to the facility down in San Diego and sat with a designer as he worked on the logo. I remember each beat so vividly. He went to dafont.com and downloaded a "komika" font pack, thinking my brand was a bit cartoonish.

It was. I loved it.

He then arranged the font and some symbols on the shoe mock. I noted he was using Adobe Illustrator, because whatever apps I had were not capable of what I watched this man do.

When I got back to North Dakota, I pirated every app I saw in use while I was at Pony. Many of them I had never heard of, because only in-house creatives really owned them at the time. The creative suite, final cut, all of it. The learning curve was steep, but a month later I had recreated the designs I had seen at Pony. I was ready to take it to the next level.

I went back to the homies and told them we could really do something with this. Between the blogs which were blowing up, the videos which kept going and getting better, and the merch I was now able to (hardly) design, I figured we could make a brand. The boys were in. It would be myself, Clay, JGant, Ramy, and Brandon Walker. Brandon, the money man, laid out the terms that we would all contribute a couple thousand and have specific roles.

"They say don't start a business with your friends, but how many businesses were started by five Berkeley grads?"

I asked the group that question and got them all fired up, but no one really knew the answer. In hindsight, it's a lot. We were not special in that way.

Soon we were off and running a full clothing llc. It was a crazy amount of work, especially in 2008, but we were young and motivated. I was in-season year-round at that point and always gone, but still running the show. There were camps, summer league, season, overseas stints, practices, media, and whatever else, and I did it all while I was also designing clothes, doing the boomtho website, crating purchase orders, shooting and editing videos, setting up brand partnerships, and writing for two blogs.

In a matter of a year I launched this brand, learned multiple creative suite apps, wrote like 50 blogs, produced 20 music videos, and led the league in rebounding, earning second team all D-League honors for my on-court efforts.

Off the court, everything was a fucking party. Everything. We may have been the actual best at it. For some kids with no money, no one had more life, hype, or swagger than us. Nobody. People could afford more props and shit that made it seem like they could do it like us, but even those paled in comparison to ours, especially once I created Mr BOOMTHO.

Mr BOOMTHO, to my knowledge, was the first ever mascot based on someone's real face: mine. I know Rob Dyrdek did it too around the same time, but I believe I was first. I wasn't famous, or a college team, or calling from inside the house, yet I had a head I could put on and become an 8 foot tall party God. We were untouchable.

In the Summer of 2011, everything went stratospheric. I came back from my first season in Korea and finally had cash y'all. This was when everything got awesome and also went wrong. There was no longer the equal investment from the group, I started throwing in more and more cash so we could build bigger and bigger. This wasn't actually a bad move, because almost every move I made hit big.

I brought back the high quality slap bracelet. Everyone wanted one. I made retro metal lunch boxes to sell our hats in. I paid for us to have space at Agenda and Magic. I expanded our line and hired both a showroom and a PR firm. Our sales were encouraging enough that we had to keep taking these measures to ensure we didn't die. In our best year, we were in 35-40 stores nationwide, and earned about 108k. The costs to achieve that were 107k. Fashion is ass, really.

I can't complain about the spending, though. The social cache that came with having BOOMTHO as a brand was unreal. I'd walk my way-too-big ass into any club, bar, party, coddamn bridal shower, whatever, dressed in a theme I had invented with a BOOMTHO license plate turned chain hanging from my neck and with a mascot head on and nobody would have an issue with it. If anything, they welcomed it. We started meeting spicier ladies and getting invited to cooler shit.

There was one time I was at a pool party at the Roosevelt hotel. I had just invented the SUNDAY FUNDAY shirt (I did) and we were all rocking them. Like seven of us, no one under 6'3", in neon tank tops popping bottles at the Tropicana Bar.

I got a text that XIV, an open air Sunday Funday party was going off and that the theme that week was 'neon.' So we pivoted and took like 20 people over to XIV.

When we arrived, we had to join a table that was already occupied and share it with the current patrons. I'd done this enough times that I knew the rules. I approached the other dude who was paying.

"I just want to let you know that everyone in a BOOMTHO shirt is gonna stay on our side. We have vodka so don't worry about us."

"Bro I spent like 70k last night," the guy who started to look surprisingly like Zuckerberg started, "I don't give a fuck."

He then ordered 25 Magnum bottles of Ace of Spades Rose and handed one to every one of us. His crew, our crew, everyone. He then started spraying them. We all did. That was the vibe of XIV, but usually only the assholes did it. He knighted all of us The Assholes this day.

I say all this because everyone thought I was the one who made that happen. I had just walked in and then the bottles started a minute later. We were all seven feet tall and had five women with us we weren't even interested in. I had shaken the server's hand. We were all wearing neon Sunday Funday tank tops that popped so much color off our skin.

No one even noticed that it was pump-fake Zuck spending $200k. They thought it was me.

"BOOMTHO?" Marlon Wayans stopped me on my way to the bathroom. "That's you?"

He was with some dude from the Chargers.

"Nobody's doing it how y'all doing it," dude from the Chargers said.

While the parties hit all time highs, the business was going off the rails.

There were so many mistakes we made simply because we didn't have experience, but the ones we made that had no excuses used to frustrate me. It came to head when we had to get a resellers permit to sell on printed blanks. One of the guys was supposed to do this. He didn't. Someone else was supposed to be researching musicians, and here I was up at 3am in Korea looking up Logic and Mac Miller and shit (it was 2012), going into practice tired.

By this point, I was perennially competing for the championship on the court. I was fully in my prime as an athlete, but dying of exhaustion trying to run this ship from overseas.

Not only that, but I was starting to get jealous, too. I'd do all the labor, and the BOOMTHO team got to enjoy the fruits. This was especially difficult during the trade shows. I'd pay for the booth and all the clothes, do the designs, contact the folks, etc, and the guys would just get to show up and take pictures with French Montana and Juelz

Santana. Further, I'd send girlfriends out, and guys would try to get at them. I'd be in Korea getting reports of foul play while trying to decompress after dropping 25 and 15 in a game earlier that night. It wasn't healthy at all.

One spring day in 2014, I sent an email calling someone out, and that was the beginning of the end. I probably should have worded it differently, but I just couldn't keep this up. It was the first time in my life I really couldn't keep going and I'd have to choose between basketball and BOOMTHO. I chose myself, like I always have, and I let BOOMTHO go.

Weirdly, that was like letting go of my innocence. BOOMTHO tethered me to the reality of my friends a bit, we always moved as one. I need to make it clear that they weren't bad guys. They are and were my best friends. They did the exact same thing I would have done, honestly. They enjoyed the hell out of themselves and I enjoyed it with them. But once that tether was gone, I was able to take parties to a whole other level, leaving the team behind.

BOOMTHO was replaced by "PLEASE SEND NUDES," an obvious sign I was starting to feel myself a little too hard. And then I went all out...

COACHELLA

In the spring of 2014, my team was playing for the championship again. Yea, we were real good out there. By that point in my career, I was not only considered the best in the country and one of the best in Asia, but my teams were pretty much a lock to win it all each season.

It's an interesting thing to be the frontrunner every year, because the games are hard, man. Each series, each moment, everything is very hard. It's like yea, we won at the end, but there were 2000 times during the season where we all believed it was over.

This season was the most trying of my life. I was in my second season as a member of Ulsan Mobis Phoebus, the best and most abusive team in Korea. On the good side, Mobis had a good mix of young and veteran talent. They also played a very smart, high movement style of basketball, combined with fast defense. They were as close to the Spurs as a Korean organization could get.

On the bad side, the head coach was more of a Bobby Knight than a Greg Popovich, the team lived on a Hyundai plant, and the physical demands of playing with them were crazy. From the day we arrived at training camp, two things were clear: we were definitely winning it all, and that to do so (from their perspective) would require me to fully hate my life.

We had apartments in Yongin, about 40 minutes outside of Seoul, but they purposefully didn't pay for air conditioning, so in mid August I had no choice but to sleep in the dorms. That seems small, but Korea in August is way too hot and humid to sleep without AC. No other team withholds AC. That's a power move.

The dorms are exactly what they sound like, except they're attached to the practice facility. All Korean teams have them, but Americans are generally exempt from staying inside. It's like if the Lakers were forced to sleep in tiny rooms inside the El Segundo facility so that they could be ready to practice morning, noon and night, year round.

That was just during camp. Once the season started, we were either in hotel rooms on the road, or staying at the Hyundai plant in Ulsan. This is an important note because many teams, including ours, decided to set up shop near Seoul, even if the team's hometown was elsewhere. It's like if every team in the NBA lived and practiced in San Francisco, and then flew to Miami, Brooklyn, or Milwaukee for their home games. If there was a long home stand, we could be on the plant for weeks.

The reason we stayed on the plant is because we were on Team Hyundai, as in the actual car company. I thought there would be some cool benefit to that, but there was not. Instead of big season ending bonuses, they offered us 25% off of a Hyundai, but with the Korean sticker price it was more expensive than in the US.

"Mobis" is in the engineering division of Kia and Hyundai. So Ulsan is full of engineers from all over the world, living and working on a plant that produces hella cars (and smog), only ever going home to their families during holiday breaks. They all wore these blue jumpsuits like mechanics might wear, they would all get up and go to work at the same time in the morning, and all end work at the same time at night. That shit was surreal. I know all of this, again, because we were right there with them. I think there were close to 10,000 men at this facility, our 20 guys making up part of that number.

There was one way in and one way out, and the coaches knew this and monitored that exit. They held a belief that every team I ever played for held: that sex took away from a player's ability to play well, so no wives or girlfriends were allowed inside the area. We weren't allowed to do anything social. When we were there, my life was basketball games, chilling at the Hyundai plant, sleeping, repeating. To make it somewhat more manageable, I'd wear a big puffy coat and walk to the market for some whiskey, smuggling it back into the plant inside the XXXXL portions of the jacket. By the end of the season there were 12 bottles hidden in my closet.

Despite all these things, we were winning. It's kinda weird winning so many games and going back home into misery, but that's how things were. Our days were very regimented. Every single morning, no matter what, we had to go down for breakfast at 7am. Then there was a break before practice at 10. Then lunch at 12. Then practice at 4. Then dinner at 7. Then film at 9. Then a late snack at 10. Literally that was my day every day for years. I feel traumatized even writing this shit out.

But you could leave the plant, right?

Wrong. Case in point, we had a half-Korean on our team named Greg Stevenson. Half Korean is an important distinction because they were usually just Americans with some Korean lineage. The bad part is they were treated much worse than anyone else, just for being half. The good part was they played like Americans and the rosters could only hold two 'Americans.' Guys like him were gold.

As a result, Greg was one of the best players in the league and a key part of everything we did. He was like the x-factor no one else had, slashing and scoring from the mid-range like no other.

Well Greg, who was 35 at the time, was married and his wife was pregnant with their second child. We had a game and she went into labor during the game. When the game was over, we all came back to the plant to be miserable, but Greg went to the hospital to sleep beside his wife and newborn baby. The next morning, the coach loudly kicked him off the team with terrible english:

"S–E–A–S–O–N O–U–T! SEASON OUT!" He spelled it and said it. He was just good enough at English to be a dick.

"Season out" meant greg was done. Only after all of us begged and pleaded for ten days did the coach let Greg back on the team. That, and hours of Greg running laps around the top level of the arena while we practiced. He couldn't just be sorry. He had to show just how sorry he was.

The crazy part is the coaches didn't even abide by any of these rules. They, like most Korean coaches, would be out getting completely shit faced every single night. No. I mean it. Every. Single. Night. We could hear them going out or coming in late in the morning, in large part because the plant was so quiet at night.

Their full volume drunken conversations going on outside in the parking area would be so loud that they would wake me up at times. The head coach loved to get the assistants drunk and make them hit each other. They would be hammered, barely standing, and the head coach would have them stand face to face and take turns slapping one another for his amusement. Can you imagine watching all of this go down through prison bars, past freshly bloomed Cherry Blossoms on a Hyundai plant at 4am? Neither could I before it happened.

He didn't just have coaches hit one another, he would hit players all the time. He once kicked our best player in the leg, leading him to get a hematoma and miss significant time. My teammate's crime? Miscommunication on a rebound. Another time, and you can google this, my coach made my teammate put athletic tape over his own mouth mid game so that he couldn't talk back (he wasn't talking back). My teammate's crime? A rebound fell through his hands. It was wild.

By the end of the season, I was tired of this shit. At the end of every season I was fully ready to leave the country, but in 2014 I wanted my ticket booked for the minute the final game was over. That was always the plan, but I had never been more serious. I wasn't staying a day, an hour, a minute longer than was necessary.

When the playoff schedule came out, I noticed something interesting. The finals had some weird schedule timing that might allow me to not only get right out of the country, but I could potentially attend Coachella. All we had to do was win the finals in 6 games are less, or lose before then. I'm a gamer, so losing wasn't an option. I decided that my light at the end of the tunnel would be a potential Coachella trip when it was all over.

When we made the finals, I started telling the homies that it was possible. This wasn't just for hubris reasons. Every single dickhead back in LA was asking me every day what my plans were. I was Mr PLEASE SEND NUDES, after all. Some people's Coachella plans didn't start until mine did, so I had to alert them that I would be the last one to make plans.

I even posted about it on Facebook. I told the fam that the series was 3-2 and that if we won the next game, I'd be able to book a flight that took off hours after the game ended. I went on to explain that that flight would land me in LA at 10am on Friday, and that I could then drive directly to Coachella in time to see Outkast bomb. It was ambitious as hell, but it was possible.

Well, the Korean media picked up on this. I didn't even think about Facebook being a platform Koreans might pull news from. Regardless, they went apeshit for this information. I was unaware, but as we were playing game 6, the commentators kept mentioning my plan as the game was unfolding.

"Benson scores two. He must really want to go to Coachella!"

I'm being serious. They made the whole game a Coachella or bust situation, which it was, but they didn't know what I had been through all season. They didn't know the pain of the plant or that the coach hit people. They just knew I wanted to party, which made it funny.

At the end of the game, I got a steal and a dunk to seal it. We were definitely going to win the championship. As I was doing a chin up on the rim after the dunk, the announcers were screaming "Benson's going to Coachella! Benson's going to Coachella!"

The only reason I know this is because my folks who speak Korean sent me messages after the game asking how the announcers knew about the Coachella plans. I truly didn't know, but it was legendary.

When I actually did go to Coachella and everyone was partying, friends would ask me how the season went.

"Won that chip," was the only answer anyone cared about.

EMAILS FROM BILL

From BILL

To: mobis

Thu, Nov 13, 2014 at 7:00 PM

Mobis Basketball Club

Dear Mobis

Please understand that this letter will serve as a formal complaint. I have copied the League.

Rodrique Benson, a professional basketball player, is still employed by your Club. He was asked to travel on a plane to his home on September 22, 2014. However, he was never properly terminated so we assume he is still employed. Pursuant to the contract he signed with your Club, Section 10.3 states 'Termination of this Agreement by Club pursuant to this Section 10.1 and Section 10.2 shall be effected by sending of written notice to Player in accordance with Section 12.5.' No notice was ever sent to either Benson or his agent, William D. Neff, me. We can only assume that no notice was sent so that the Mobis club could keep his rights to potentially trade him. Or, the Mobis club does not believe in following rules. Whatever the case may be, the Club owes Mr. Benson $75,000 and the clock ticks each day.

Mr. Neff, his agent, has not been paid the second half of his agent fee or $14,823. Mr. Neff was to receive his first payment within 15 days after the issuance of the working visa and the second payment within 7 days of the Player being regis-tered in the KBL. Both were done months ago but Mr. Neff still has not been paid.

I request immediate payment for both with penal-ties and interest.

I understand that the Club is taking steps to not allow Mr. Benson to return to Korea to play in the future because of their mistaken belief that we were looking for an under the table payment. Personally, that is slanderous to me, a non-public figure, and I will look into my legal rights in this country because of the way this Club is defaming me. Never in my 22 years of doing business have I asked for an under the table payment. They have no proof. As we did not understand the rules yet, we asked for certain things and they said they could not do them. Once the rules were explained, we asked again and again for win bonuses if the Club won the Champi-onship, Section 2.2. They gave Mr. Benson the least they could. As Section 2.2 states, 'In addition to the Base Compensation, Club may, at its sole discretion and at any time after September 2014 during the Term, pay incentive to Player in an amount determined by Club.' We wanted to maximize that amount. I can provide those emails whenever you would like. Further, under Section 2.1.6, the Club could have given extra incentive but they did not. That is what we were asking for. At Mr. Benson's last meeting with the Club, they kept writing down instances of what they perceived were his receipts of other incentives from previous Clubs. Mobis gave him a gift card last year which was not in his agreement, similar to what other clubs had given him, after wins.

This concept of Mr. Benson looking for under the table payments began at the draft two years ago when it was thought he would be the first round pick. He asked me, his agent, to tell some of the clubs he would prefer not to be drafted by their team as they had no chance to win and he wanted bonus money. I went first to Calvin Oldham of KCC and he listened and drafted another player. Prior to the second pick, I went to Duane Ticknor of LG and asked him to not pick him as he would not make enough bonus money. LG complained that I asked for under the table money which I did not. LG drafted him, anyway, and Ticknor later apologized to me. I would not know how to do an under the table deal. Mr. Benson just wants to maximize his income during his short career as a basketball player. That night, the League defamed me but I left it alone but now, with this allegation by Mobis, you are hurting my earning power while obviously hurting Mr. Benson's. I will not let

Mobis get away with their choosing to enforce rules when it benefits them but ignoring others which do not enrich them.

In conclusion, I ask for an understanding of Mr. Benson's situation with Mobis, immediate payment of the debts owed to Mr. Benson and me, his agent, and finally, I ask your Club to cease and desist the unfounded character assassination of Mr. Benson. As I said, I will exhaust all legal remedies because we do follow rules, have always followed rules and are disgusted that the Mobis team completely ignores them.

END OF DISCUSSION

It was near the end of my junior year of high school that I got my first basketball recruitment letter. I had been heavily recruited in volleyball, which meant sporadic letters from UCLA, USC, and Pepperdine, but as a JV dude, there was no way I would get letters for basketball.

I started playing AAU for the first time that spring, and we were getting clobbered nearly every game, so it was crazy that I got a letter from Yale. I think their strategy was to plant as many seeds as possible. I assume they send out thousands of letters a year. Still, I had mine. The Torrey Pines head coach handed it to me, almost in jest, and I immediately started bragging to the homies.

"You're not good enough to play at Yale, Rod," one of them said before pushing me over a bench.

Maybe we weren't that close?

Undeterred, I stared at it for hours before I opened it. I sat it on my desk in Honors Physics and just looked at it instead of paying attention. I was used to looking at the UCLA volleyball letters, but Yale Basketball was on another level. When I got home, my mom felt the same way.

"You're going to Yale."

"Mom," I pleaded, "it's just a letter. I'm not even good. They're not even good!"

"You're going to Yale. End of discussion."

It really was the end of the discussion.

FUCK IS THAT GUY?

The University of California at Berkeley is rivals with Stanford. I'm unsure how many people know that since it's Berkeley and Cal aren't allowed to call themselves the same thing, legally. But yes, when Cal played Stanford in the early 2000s it was some heated shit. If someone wore a red shirt to ANY Cal sporting event, the entire crowd would yell "take off that red shirt!" This would last either until the person went shirtless or left. My freshman year, Cal won The Big Game for the first time in a decade and students marched the goal posts down the boulevard. I was in Cleveland walking backwards through a blizzard so I missed it.

In basketball we were good, but for some bitch ass reason, Stanford was a nationally ranked top 5 team for most of my time in college. It was kinda dope though because I can say a) I played against the #1 team in the country multiple times between Stanford, Arizona, and Washington and b) the crowds were always super lit for these games, especially against Stanford.

The first time we played at Stanford was some wild shit. Everyone knew and openly talked about how Stanford had springs under the floor so you could jump higher. I'm unsure if that's the exact reason, but you could definitely fly at Stanford my freshman year. What was both jarring and cool was that the student body knew this too, so when we would shoot free throws, they would all jump at once, like 8000 people, and the entire court would move like a rolling wave and make the baskets shake 8 inches side to side.

I know I'm doing a lot of hyping Stanford, but I'm not really. I'm hyping the feeling that we created by caring so much. The pinnacle of that feeling came my junior season when I was the team's leading scorer. We were at Stanford (they had changed the floor by then), and the arena was sold out. It was a big ass game. So big, in fact, that Tiger Woods was there sitting court side. Let me say this again, Tiger Motherfucking Woods sat court side to watch us play basketball in 2005. May as well have been light skinned cablinasian Jesus.

Well, we were down 8-10 or something in the second half at one point. This timing and score happened often in college. If you can't get past 8, you could stay around a 10 point deficit for the rest of the game. Knowing this, I tried to go atomic to keep us in it. Mind you, "atomic" for me wasn't like Kobe or whatever you're thinking, but my version. Either way, I scored 4 straight buckets on four consecutive possessions, no free throws. On the third bucket, Tiger made a confused face like " who the fuck is that guy?"

Of course I was looking at him and clocked this.

Nice.

On the fourth make, I looked again and he did three slow nods and looked me in the eye. He knew I was a gamer and he let me know.

HOOLLYYY SHITTT.

Literally the single greatest acknowledgement of my basketball abilities ever. Tiger gave me three nods during a sell out at Stanford. Y'all can't tell me shit.

I think I missed every shot the rest of the game.

MINICAMPS 2

I made the Sacramento Kings summer league roster off the strength of my minicamp performance. I honestly don't remember what happened, because I was out of breath for most of it, but at the end some very old man that everyone respected pulled me aside and shook my hand. He told me I surprised him with my whatever-it-was and asked if I'd be interested in playing for the Kings that summer.

Hell yea my guy.

As the date approached for summer league, the Kings hired Eric Musselman. A coaching change is always a concern, but my agent was sure nothing had changed for us. I guess it was known that that old man was the king maker (yea, a pun) and had final say. So I told everyone that I would be in Vegas and that they could meet me there in mid July.

The Kings sent me the itinerary and $100 per diem for the first day. They put me up in the Embassy Suites in Sac, which was my first time staying at one. That shit was nice for a man of my means. I was too excited. I spent $50 of my per diem on a steak dinner. I wanted to be well fed and ready if I was gonna go into the facility ready for action.

When we arrived at the arena the next day, guys were getting taped up. This was a surprise because the itinerary said we were going directly to the airport. Scratch that. There was a pile of fresh Kings practice gear sitting on a chair with my name on it, so I buckled in and got ready to go hard. This was my first surprise mini-camp.

Instead of going hard, I essentially watched 20 other D-leaguers practice. I was pulled from every drill and did none of the competitive stuff. Although it was my first time hearing it, I knew this song and dance. When it was over, Musselman pulled myself and a few other guys aside.

"Thanks for coming out guys. We aren't going to need you," he said, walking away during the last couple of words.

I looked at the other guys, including Odartey Blankson who just shrugged. I guess I would now have to find my way home. That was a tough ask, considering I had $34 left after that dumb ass steak dinner and a Jamba Juice.

Everyone I knew was going to Vegas to meet me, and I was as embarrassed as I've ever been. Even if none of the terrible shit was real, the fact that I was actually just not good enough to be one of twenty guys to make the fucking Kings summer league roster was an excellent reminder that it can always get worse.

I showered and parked myself in the lobby of the facility.

DAFUQ I'M SUPPOSED TO DO NOW?

I told one person I was cut from the Kings, and that was my boy Sam. Sam was a freshman manager on the basketball team, turned cool dude and lifelong friend. I had slept on Sam's floor, both at his frat in Berkeley and his parents house in Eugene, Oregon. So when I called Sam and he told me he was going to go see a band from his high school that night, I asked if I could join. I also asked if it was free. I didn't want to be alone, and somehow it felt comforting to go kick it with Eugene people, even if most of them were strangers. But it had to be free. The Rib Eye got me. He said it was.

I used 22 of the 34 available dollars to buy a train ticket from Sacramento to San Francisco and met Sam at a venue to watch my first ever rock show. The band was called "Rock and Roll Soldiers" and I loved their music right away. This was mostly because they had a song on "Smallville" called "Funny Little Feeling" that kinda slapped.

I sat there in the balcony with Sam, drinking whatever drink he paid for, watching this Eugene based band play songs. I was doing everything except checking into The Venetian with the Kings.

After the show was over, the guys came backstage and they were all very cool folks. We chopped it up like we had all been friends for years. They all went to South Eugene High School, a place Sam had shown me and the high school of my then girlfriend, Maria. Everyone knew everyone. It was the hug I needed after a very long day.

The next morning I woke up in a stuffy San Francisco apartment. The first thing I saw was a half eaten burrito sitting right in front of my face.

How did I afford this burrito?

Wait.

I should eat this burrito.

When I was finished with the burrito, I looked around the room. Everyone was asleep in some awkward fashion. Comforters and feet were everywhere. Odd though. For how many people were there, Sam was the obvious one missing. I grabbed my phone to text him but he had already texted me.

> Had to bounce. Guys are cool. Talk later.

I looked back up at the waking Rock and Roll Soldiers. Everyone looked pretty rough so I assumed I must also look pretty rough as well.

"We gotta leave now if we're going to make good time," one of them said.

OH SHIT. I'M STILL BROKE. I'M SUPPOSED TO BE IN VEGAS.

"Oh yea. Ha. I'm still broke. I guess I should figure my life out," I said, trying to think of how to tell my mom to not meet me in Vegas. Maybe she had already started driving. This was bad.

"Bro, why don't you come with us! We're just going to Eugene. Isn't Maria there?"

"Damn you're right she is. But she's at the country faire or some shit. I'm unsure she's available."

"Well, whatever man. I think you should just come up. Why the fuck not, right?"

Other members of the band were starting to chime in. The chorus was growing louder and more effective.

"You should definitely do it man! Let's go!"

It was both too loud for 8am and just loud enough to convince me. I was in. It really didn't take much. I had literally nothing else in life that was going to demand my time and attention. So when we started driving up the I80 in a 15 passenger van full of equipment, no one cried foul. It wasn't the action I expected, but I was now, again, ready for action.

As we got on the Bay Bridge, I noticed a billboard. It read:

"Are you? Gay.com"

I thought the phrasing was funny.

"Do people need help knowing? I feel like you would know. Shit, I guess anyone can start a website about anything these days," I announced.

That was a very 2006 statement.

"Yea, I don't get it. I don't even know what I would make a website about," a soldier said.

"Me either but it'll be better than areyougay.com that's for sure," I asserted, like a man who had extensive web and gay experience.

It was about an hour north of Santa Rosa that the alcohol began to wear off. The car started to feel hot, and although there were only 8 people, it was also too stuffy and full. Nobody had the same energy as they did earlier. It was just a boring car ride at that point. That's when it hit me for real.

This could be dumb.

It was.

I decided I needed to call Maria, because this could get out of hand very quickly. Where would I even stay? Why did I think this was a good idea? I needed answers, so I picked up the phone and I called. No answer. Again. No answer. One more time. No answer.

CODDAMN COUNTRY FAIRE.

I then tried her mom. I knew she was at the faire as well, but maybe there was slightly more accessibility through her? It was worth a shot.

"Rod!" Her mom picked up on the first ring.

"Hey! How is it over there?"

"Rod!"

"Hello!"

"Rod!"

I couldn't tell if she couldn't hear me or if the drugs were hitting, but the phone call was meaningless. That's no judgment, either. She had never done or mentioned drugs around me. But people were telling me that the faire was essentially just a mushroom fest in the forest and that no one attends it sober, so it was the only answer I could tell myself. Everyone was getting in my head. We were now just a couple hours outside of Eugene and I was running out of options. I called Sam to see if he knew what I should do.

"You know the South guys out there. You should call them," he said matter of factly.

He's always so matter of fact. He was right, though. He had other friends from his high school days that I had met many times in my trips to Eugene. Four of them lived together in a house, but because it was summer break, the house was relatively open, save for one guy. Sam gave me his number and I called him. He told me I could come down to the house, so that became my plan.

When I arrived at the house, it was dark. I'm unsure what time it was, but it was definitely bed time. The Soldiers wished me luck and dropped me off. I forget the dude's name at the house, but he was nice enough about the whole situation. He walked me to some guy's room and I closed the door. I didn't even have bags. I picked up the phone and rang Maria a few more times. There was no answer, so I went to bed.

It was a weird four days at the house. Weird might be an understatement. I didn't have money. I didn't have a car. I was too embarrassed to tell anyone that I wasn't in Las Vegas, and yes they were asking. I just kind of laid in that bedroom alone and ashamed for days.

On the fourth night, she called. I've never felt more relief in my whole life.

"Rod! Are you in Eugene?!"

"Uhh… Yeupppp."

"Oh my God I'm going to come get you right now!"

She picked me up in her mom's car and drove me to her parents house as I explained everything. At every turn of the story she was more shocked than the last. I had almost forgotten that I hadn't seen her actual face since school ended a month earlier. There wasn't FaceTime or Zoom. It was as much a reunion as it was a rescue.

When we got to her house, I kept explaining everything and she put on "A Beautiful Mind." That movie was so damn sad that I almost forgot where I was. I don't know when, but I fully stopped talking and I got immersed in that film.

When it ended I was spinning, but shit, I had to make a move. Nothing to cure loneliness like horniness, but I was rejected when I made a play.

I looked at her, confused. She looked away and then back.

"I never said we were still together."

"You never said we weren't!"

I don't remember the rest of the words, but I do remember being dropped back off at that house and going back into that room and closing the door. I thought I wasn't capable of a real cry, but I was very wrong. That cry was like the river nile. I don't know if I slept and dreamed I kept crying or if I didn't sleep and just cried. Either way, I just kept on cryin'.

It took three days to get the courage to tell Bill that I wasn't in Las Vegas.

"Yes. I'm aware," he said, which seemed to replace the question 'where are you?' and hit the same. Of course he was aware.

He booked me a train ticket to Portland and a flight to get back to San Diego. Before we got off the phone I had one more request.

"What's that, Boomptho?"

"Can you get me a MacBook? I know it's expensive."

"Why?"

"I wanna start a website. I saw a billboard an–"

"Done."

And on the train from Eugene to Portland, armed with my new white MacBook, I bought the domain toomuchrodbenson.com and started writing this story out for the very first blog entry. Areyougay.com be damned.

CREAM

The 2011-2012 season was crazy. We came into the season as the #1 ranked team in Korea and lived up to it in every single way. This was my second season out there and the rules had dramatically changed. The season before, each Korean team could have two Americans, but could only play one at a time. This season, however, each team just had one and the pay was doubled.

All the hype was that with the doubled pay, teams could recruit NBA level talent. There was some speculation that Dongbu made a mistake in keeping me. With a larger talent pool, was I actually worth money that could go to dudes who had just come off league contracts? Yes. The answer was yes. We fucked all these teams up.

A big part of the reason we did so well was that we were a coddamn unit. I knew how to work with my guys better than everyone else. It was me, Yun Ho Young, and Kim Joo Sung. They called us the "triple tower," in large part because we played this crazy junk defense that took a ton of brain power but led us to a ton of blocked shots.

The architect, head coach Kang Dong Hee, kept giving us spicer game plans and we knocked them out of the park. I posit there are still dudes from that season who think I'm trash and was just "on a good team."

They're the type of guys who give takes on ESPN and you wonder if they ever knew the game. They didn't.

That's not to say that they weren't fucking good at basketball. I was challenged every game by my matchups for sure. It's crazy (and sad) that three of the guys who gave me the most trouble have since passed. Jackson Vroman, Chris Williams, and Jasper Johnson. 3 out of 16. Crazy.

Anyways, we kept rolling that season. We broke team records for wins, margin of victory, longest winning streak, and I won MVP. We were so hot that they invited my ass to appear on Gag Concert, essentially SNL for Koreans. We were "rock stars" so to speak.

Fast forward and we were tied 2-2 in the KBL finals. It didn't make any sense to me. We had beaten the opponents, KGC, 5 of 6 times that season and had set many of our records against them. In this series, however, the games were hard and close. It was tiring as all hell because Anyang has horrible air quality. Kang Dong Hee suddenly couldn't put together a game plan or make the right subs. I started coaching us in some situations because everything was falling apart. But nothing was worse than the refs. These dudes were absolutely fucking us.

My anger was rising after each missed call. I know that as a basketball player, I/we complain about nearly every play so I was legitimately confused when the refs actually seemed to be on their side. Game after game. Home and on the road. It was clear.

Late in the game, down one, I went up after a post move and I was fouled by three different people. They were intentionally trying to foul me because I only shot 69% from the line and it was safer than letting me have a layup. The refs called nothing. I grabbed my headband, which had been knocked off during the play, and threw it into the stands. Tech. I then made some big gestures. Tech two, ejected. Fine by me.

I completely lost it. I ripped my jersey off and threw it. I, while dragging multiple teammates, went to each ref and cussed each of them out in very mean and personal ways. After ten minutes of holding the game up, I was on my way out of the arena when the best player on KGC did a throat slash at me. I charged back in and did another 5 minutes on stage. It was as performative as it was adrenaline fueled.

I thought I was going to get kicked out of the league. Guys have done less and been banned for life. I was not, however, because of the breaking news. My coach, Kang Dong Hee, was arrested for match fixing. Not only was he fixing matches, he was tanking OUR games. I guess the money on the finals was at its highest levels, so that's why he went dumb during timeouts and subs. Further, the refs were in on it. They were all fired. Literally an entire new set of refs took over the next season, and they added a two minute report and all kinds of stuff because no one had faith that the sport was above board.

The shitty part is there was no retribution for shit. KGC won and got the trophy. I lost out on $30k in bonus money and salary, not to mention a big hit to my legacy as a loser. There were huge conse-quences for those actions. The corporations involved with the teams all knew what was happening and didn't care, nor were they punished for that inaction. The thousands of sports books littered throughout Korea and the sports networks pushing the betting sites all day long — I assume they got paid as well. When I turn on ESPN these days and 3/4 of the screen reads DRAFT KINGS this is where my mind goes.

It was extra fucked up because the local politicians all knew what Kang was up to. They would all be at team dinners with us all the time, speaking in private and sharing Soju. Often they would be joined by the local mobsters who ran the sports books and networks. Yes, mobsters who were literally known for burying people in the desert. Millions of dollars being moved around by people at every level. It was all in the open and the only people who really got fucked were the players and fans. Honestly, with all that support, Kang would have dumb not to bet on our games.

I know what you're thinking: "that's crazy! So corrupt!"

All I've learned after getting screwed in a similar fashion by basketball teams across the globe, fashion brands and PR firms, nonprofits and huge chains, the apartment I rent from and the HOA when I owned, even best friends and the maintenance man down the hall is: every single person in a position of power who can cheat, does at some point. Some do it consistently for years, some do it once and feel bad and try to be better, but they all do it. I literally have friends who purposefully over charge on everything from solar panels to insurance. There are some exceptions, like the fine folks at the PGA *rolls eyes*, but no matter how much money you think is involved, there's always way more. ALWAYS. WAY. MORE.

Due to the expected nature of all this lying, cheating, and manipulation, people don't really care about those circumstances when judging one another's success. It's binary. Did you overcome it and win or not? No one cares how it happened. LeBron losing to the Pistons means a finals loss. The end. KD injured against the Raptors. Doesn't matter. Kawhi is now a legend.

2012, another year in the books that can be summarized as another year Dongbu didn't win. Benson's now 0-2 in the finals. Maybe Rod Benson isn't worth the high price tag.

TALK ABOUT IT.

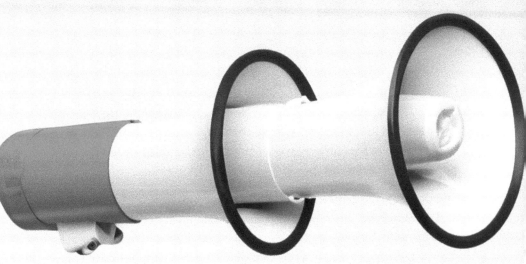

Oh shit. You got the takes so hot, not even Jesus could cool them off!

No?

Oh word. You grew up near an eventual all-star and now you want to levearge that relationship? Not you?

Well then shit, you can still go to journalism school get a beat with the college team, then the local pro, then the whatever.

Oh. You played the game? That means you have the best takes, who cares if you never learned the plays?

Or!

You could do TMZ! Either way the narrartive is yours!

DD
DIFFERENT DUDE™

LESBIAN ANYWAYS

When I got to college, we were given our lockers almost right away. This was an obvious move because there was a lot of practice and, as freshmen, there was no way we were going to be able to keep up with laundry and everything.

One thing they specifically wanted us to keep up with was showering. LISTEN. I needed this phase very badly. I had a very complicated relationship with hygiene at that age, so when they told us we had to shower after every single event we did, I wasn't happy. I didn't like being dirty, but I damn sure did enjoy being lazy.

When the coaches first made a big deal out of showering, I knew I had to figure out my own smell situation for sure. When they made it a big deal every day and added specifics, it got weird.

Bear in mind, at age 17 and 18 and with no memberships to exclusive health clubs among us, none of us had ever showered in front of another man before. Not a single one of us. So when practice was over, everyone else would shower and the freshmen would linger around, waiting for everyone else to finish so we could have the entire shower area to ourselves. As far as the staff was concerned, this was unacceptable.

We were told there would be consequences for not showering among one another, and there were. We would routinely lose access to our locker room for not showing in front of everyone else. It was kind of wild.

To be sure, the only reason we were hesitant was homophobia. I can only really speak for myself, but being skinny, smiley, and smart as a black man led many to call me gay. It was so dumb, looking back on it, but it became a big fear of mine. I was already struggling to get female attention, the last thing I needed was another obstacle. Plus, as an athlete, there was something extra about being perceived gay that made it seem like you could be dominated in-game. It wasn't right, but I processed all these thoughts every time they told me I HAD to get into the shower with my naked male teammates.

I resisted as long as I could. We all did. I really think eventually the punishments were too much to bear and we capitulated. We all got into the shower with everyone else, meat sticks dangling to and fro. This was the first time I had seen peer penis and it was weird. It was a lot. I wasn't just seeing dick. I was seeing DICK.

You'd think this whole process would make everyone else less homophobic, but it had the exact opposite effect. With so much dick in the air, literally every look/comment/question HAD to be justified with a swift "no homo."

"Aye G, no homo, you got a bruise on your hip man."

"No homo man, I saw that. Trainer says it's all good. And for real, no gay shit, your shoulders getting big bro."

"For real! Straight as an arrow my guyyyyyy. I was thinking I've been getting hard so easily lately."

"Bro on some cis male shit, straight up. I'd never have sex with you. I love that we both know that."

"We do. On some 'if you look at my lips for longer than a second I'll send someone to kill you' because I love you type shit."

"You my nigga for that dawg, on some 'I'm a lesbian anyways' type shit."

This was literally every conversation in the shower. Any time anyone didn't start or end a sentence with "no homo" we just started saying they were gay.

U-TURN

I was walking from the hotel to the US Airways center in Phoenix, Arizona for the first day of camp with the Suns in 2009. It was something like 9am, and I recall it already being very hot and sunny. It was a pleasant feeling, the sun on my skin and the knowledge that in minutes I'd have a chance to compete for a spot on the Suns roster for good.

As I walked, I thought about who was on the roster. Who could I out maneuver? Which coaches knew my old coaches? What spot should I get dinner tonight after practice?

My phone rang and snapped me out of my daydreaming. It was my agent, Bill.

"BOOMP THO! Where are you?!" He always seemed to pronounce it with a 'p' in there.

"Hey Bill. I'm walking to the arena as we speak. Ready to get after it!"

"Stop," Bill said urgently.

"What?"

"Are you there yet?"

"No...."

"Ok then turn around and go back to the hotel. I'll call you."

I turned around and walked back to the hotel. Bill called a few minutes later.

"Head to the airport. You're going to Indy."

"To indy?!"

"Yes. Indy. Right now. Call me when you get there."

And that's how I ended up in camp with the Pacers.

MEANINGLESS WORDS

Towards the end of my rookie season in the D-League in '07, my team was in position to make the finals with one more win. With that win, not only would we be in the Finals, but the Finals would be a one game series and that game would be in Bismarck, North Dakota, our home city. No one outside of Bismarck cared about this, really, as the league was still new and most of the games (including the finals) were not televised nationally.

As it became clear we might have a chance for the finals, I decided to ask a woman I was interested in, Tracy, to come out to Bismarck to visit pending that win. If we were to lose, the timing wouldn't work out. So there was a lot riding on that semifinal. I didn't have the money to fly her out, so this trip would also incur another $800 in debt to Bill, but I didn't care. I was just hyped to have the chance to see her and win a chip in the same day.

Fast forward and we win the semis. So now I go ahead and book Tracy's flight with money I don't have and get her out to North Dakota's capital city for the championship game. That game was against the Colorado 14ers, who had a bunch of guys I was friends with. That matters because in the D-League, some cities would be so small that we would just kick it with the other team. They would be the only people in town who were like us. It was common practice.

The game was as intense as any game I've ever played. Darius Rice had 52 points on 11-17 from 3 (this was in 2007, mind you) and hit a contested 3 to send the game to overtime. It was absolutely bananas. I could see from the court that Tracy was going super hard in the stands cheering us on. It was magical. We ended up winning 129-121 in OT and became the first D-League champions in the era of expansion.

After the game, both teams went to one of the only two tiny bars in town and partied. Tracy was being slightly OD in terms of celebrating with the champions and clowning the losers, but it was actually pretty funny so no one was tripping. I have to say that, because It was kind of weird because we were drinking and taking photos with the trophy and the 14ers were in the same room just kind of sitting in it.

Everyone was sitting in it, for better or worse. All the league officials and media were also in the bar because, where else would they go? Noting like both teams, the league president, and a bunch of sportswriters packed into some tiny bar in North Dakota like a damn family reunion, drinking beers to country music while a gigantic meaningless trophy trades hands for photos (this was pre iPhone).

We soon moved the party from the bar to my apartment because bars did last call at midnight back then and we hadn't arrived til nearly 11. With last call being so early, a lot of places sold beer off sale, so we scooped up a couple cases of beer and took them with us. The officials didn't come, but many of the 14ers did.

At the crib it was pretty chill. In fact, it was way more chill than earlier. We were mostly just sitting around talking and drinking bottles of Coors and Dos Equis. There weren't any women there besides Tracy and no one was even really drinking that much anymore. It just kind of felt like we *had* to keep partying because the season was over and if we were in any other city, we would have been at a club at that hour.

I was in the kitchen area talking to a guy from the 14ers, Steve. Steve and I were having a semi-serious discussion about lord knows what. I just remember that we were pretty locked in at the moment and it felt like he and I had a lot in common, which was a rare feeling in that first year. Out of nowhere, Tracy walked up and interrupted us mid-sentence.

"Did you lose or win?" She asked, eyes half open because she was so drunk. I remember thinking that was weird phrasing so far after the game ended.

"We los-"

I can tell you that as soon as the 's' sound came out of this man's mouth, Tracy turned the bottle of beer she was drinking upside down, emptied it on his head, and walked out of the room.

"Bitch," she said as she stumbled away.

I was absolutely shook. I had no clue what to do. I assumed Steve would just try to fight me and I'd likely lose because I was more drunk and certainly much skinnier. I was also so sure that the other 14er guys remaining in the room might beat me up for what just happened. I caught myself, realizing while I was processing all this, I was just standing there staring directly at this man with my mouth wide open. I was frozen in time. Steve was livid, but seemingly also frozen in time. Neither of us said anything for long enough that I began to notice time passing.

"I'm so sorry, man. Wow." I finally mustered some meaningless words.

To his credit, Steve just looked at me.

"I think it's time to go," he said through his teeth.

I got him a towel, and helped clean up. The party was fully over at this point and I made sure everyone got out and made it back to their places safely.

After everyone was out, I realized I hadn't seen Tracy since she unapologetically walked away. The apartment was relatively big and had a long hallway, so the party area and the bed area were very separate. When I walked around and started down the hallway I was shocked at what I was seeing down the hall. The bedroom door was wide open and Tracy was laying there masturbating. Hard. She then looked up at me with angry eyes.

"You wouldn't know what to do with this. Bitch."

I closed the door and slept on the couch. We never even kissed during her stay.

PETE

I didn't learn about Pete Newell until I got to Cal, and that now feels like a shame. Everyone knows John Wooden, but no one knows that Pete Newell and John Wooden competed against one another, and that both had incredible basketball and life insights. That's not to say that Pete needs to be directly compared to Wooden, but I think that they both had such extraordinary careers, I hate that people stopped learning after they learned Wooden's story.

When I met Pete, he took a liking to me right away. He was putting us through some drills intended to help our Israeli Center, Amit Tamir. I had to be there because they needed bodies, but I was such a sponge, I may have learned more than anyone. This was the year I went Grimy, too, so once I learned the information, I became an asshole about it. Pete never seemed to care about my attitude.

One big reason for the jump between my sophomore and junior season at Cal was Pete. He invited me to his world famous Big Man Camp and I happily accepted. I don't think these exist anymore but back then they were all the rage. Pete would host 100 of the nations best big men in Hawaii for a week. Anyone who was anyone would attend and come back an All American, or so they told me.

I went and I did improve. I improved a lot. But the basketball wasn't the biggest thing to me. It was the first time I did something that felt professional. Our schools were removed from our jerseys and it was just us players. We formed friendships, saw one another's lifestyles, and learned who really had game and who didn't. I think Pete was always teaching bigger lessons.

What I didn't expect, though, was that when I headed to San Diego the week after camp, I would get a call from my high school friend, Kelly. Kelly and his brother Tommy grew up in Rancho Santa Fe, near the Morgan Run resort, and attended nearby Torrey Pines High. Kelly is one of these people who just finds himself around big basketball names, either accidentally or purposefully.

"Are you in town?" He asked in a rushed tone.

"Yea," I answered, "just at my moms in Cardiff."

"I'm at Pete Newell's house. You should come by."

I didn't realize he lived so close by. I got up and headed out to Pete Newell's condo, which just so happened to sit next to Kelly and Tommy's childhood home, on the edge of Morgan Run. When I walked in, he was happy to see me. He shook my hand and asked me to take a seat.

I can't lie. I don't remember a single story he told in the four hours we were there. Not a single one. I can also tell you this, I left there with a million dollars worth of game. Whatever he spoke about that day settled within my consciousness and never left. It was like he empowered me to stop playing basketball and start thinking basketball.

I actually think this is why every coach I had since college called me coachable. Maybe I had my moments of defiance, but when it came to the game plan, the plays, the angles, all that, I was always a step ahead of the guys I played with or against.

When my Junior season started, I was more than just a rage monster. I was thinking about the angles and the ways to gain advantages that other guys were unaware of. I added a turnaround bank off the glass and began to learn how rebounds worked. I started valuing charges as much as blocks. All of these things led me to completely change my game forever and were things coaches always valued as a pro.

Thanks, Pete.

CUT

The first time I was cut as a pro, Lawrence Frank called me into his office and thanked me for my time in New Jersey.

It felt disingenuous considering the day before I had blocked a shot that got the crowd at West Point hyped. Instead of letting the cheers continue, he made a point to stop practice, roll his eyes, and inform everyone that it was a goal tend.

The writing was on the wall.

NOT GOING TO BE ENOUGH

In the spring of 2010 right after my D-League season ended, Bill called and said he had a deal for me in the Dominican Republic. The team was already down 0-1 in the finals and had offered me $750 a day to come in on some mercenary type ish. Since I was making about that every two weeks in the D-League, it seemed like a no brainer. Two days later, I was on a red eye to Santo Domingo, DR.

They put me up in a small hotel with actual keys for the locks of the rickety doors. I threw my stuff down, and it was time to head to the gym for a game right away.

As we drove, I noticed that the neighborhood kept getting worse the closer we got to the arena. It seemed my hotel was very close to a line between the wealthy part of town and the poor part. The town turned into a slum, rife with stray dogs and shoeless citizens, and then the arena appeared. It almost seemed like it was photoshopped into the frame.

I went out and had something like 30 and 20 that night in the win. Now we were tied 1-1 in the best-of-seven series and a few things happened. First, word spread that I was in town and that the tides had turned in the series. I watched the local news back at the hotel, and even though I don't speak Spanish, when they showed me on the screen I knew they were gassing me up. Second, it was confirmed to me that the opposing team was representative of the slum area and their fans weren't happy about the result. I was told to watch my back. Seriously. And third, I realized that if I was getting paid by the day, it might behoove me to lose a game or two. I didn't do this, but I always thought it was wild to pay anyone that way without any extra winning bonus. I digress.

Game three was madness. We won, sure, but those opposing fans I mentioned went apeshit. They were throwing bottles and rocks onto the court. They were looking me dead in the eye and doing throat slashes and finger guns at me. They were shaking the arena so hard that the power went out twice for like seven minutes each. I had never seen anything like it. I went to bed that night a little worried about the lack of security in the hotel, but I got over it.

The next two games went exactly the same way. We won and I was putting up gaudy numbers. This was actually some of the best basketball I ever played in my life, before or after. I was shaking fools, hitting threes, taking off from outside the lane and banging on fools. It was wild. All of this while being pelted with water bottles and empanadas. The arena going dark for minutes. All of that.

When we did win game five and were handed the trophy, all seemed to be well. There was a parade in the streets and everything. Fools lifted me in the air while they chanted "CDP CAMPEON! CDP CAMPEON!"

The whole city came together to dance and drink. I felt like in the end, the fans were all bark and no bite. I reflected on how dope that was that they could be that crazy in the arena and cool outside of it.

The next night, my final night there, the GM called my hotel to tell me to meet him downstairs. He was going to pay me my $7500 for ten days of work. If I had lost a game... I digress.

When I got downstairs, he was waiting in an old Mitsubishi Montero and he was waving for me to get in. I climbed into the passenger seat and slid it all the way back. I turned back to him and waited.

"Have you enjoyed your time?" He asked as the car began rolling.

I nodded. I was tired.

We had a few minutes of meaningless conversation before I realized he had just been circling the block. The fourth time around, he handed me an envelope. I opened it and saw the correct amount of money. I then looked back at him and he was staring me directly in the eye.

"Be careful," he said without blinking.

I squinted.

What the hell?

"Be careful," he repeated.

It was when he said it that second time that I realized everything about the situation. I didn't know who knew that I was being paid, who knew what I was being paid, who knew where I stayed or what room, or my route to the airport the next day. In that area, $7500 may as well be a million.

I ran up to my room and locked the rickety ass knob. This was clearly not going to be enough. I then slid the entire bed, frame and all, in front of the door. This was clearly not going to be enough. I then put the money in a pillowcase and then put it in between the mattresses. This was clearly not going to be enough. I then turned off all the lights and TV. This was clearly not going to be enough, but it was all I could do.

I didn't sleep. I laid there going haywire at every sound I heard in the hallway until it was morning. I made my way out of DR the next day and landed back in LA. When I did, the homies asked me how it was out there.

"Won that chip," is all I said to them. It's the only answer that mattered anyway.

HOMIE SHIT.

Do you know a guy who plays basketall? You do? Well, you're in luck.

By lingering around that guy, you'll lead a life of riches, fame, hoes, and more! And   the best part?

You won't have any of the caveats! You can have 0 problems and 99 Bitches today!

Wait. You don't know a guy who plays? No problem! Get on Twitter and get in those mentions. It's tedious, but the rewards wikl be worth it when you're invited to the Guys Choice awards. Stay blesssed.

DD
DIFFERENT DUDE™

MUSCLE AND MELANIN

When I was in high school I was skinny as hell. I don't know if I ever weighed myself, but if I had to guess my playing weight my senior year, I'd guess it was around 180. At 6'10", that essentially amounted to a pile of sticks, bound together with very tight skin.

In games, the strategy against me was as unimaginative as it was successful: put some dude who played football in to rough me up. I always hated this, mostly because although it did slow me down, we never lost to a team that played that way. So all they did was fuck up my stats and leave me all bruised up.

That's another thing, high school referees let a lot go because they legitimately reffed games purely based on emotion. The amount of times I heard a ref say "play through it big fella I ain't gonna give you that," are enough to fill this entire book with. They always wanted to see me play like Shaq or something and I was incapable. It was always bullshit.

One night we were playing La Jolla high. Maybe it was Country Day? I don't remember. All I remember is they had a football dude who was bad at basketball named Will Peddy. Will must have been 6'5", 300 lbs, and it was known he was going to UCLA on a football scholarship.

NATURALLY this was my match up. Naturally I was getting abused. Naturally, the refs were "not gonna give [me] that."

At this age, I was still learning how to be a physical player, so I was unsure how to hit someone like that. I wanted to hit him back so badly but I didn't know how to execute without getting ejected. I just had to figure out a way to hit this man back or I was likely to end the game with half my sticks broken.

One of my teammates got fouled and went to the free throw line. It then dawned on me that if I stood next to Peddy, I might be able to elbow him in the natural motion of the rebound. So I lined up next to him in a normal rebounding position with my arms straight up. He wasn't paying attention. Why would he? He was safe. Except he wasn't.

BOOOOOOM

My right elbow went straight into Peddy's mouth, knocking him back. My hands were straight up, signaling I hadn't led with an elbow. How could it be a foul? It wasn't because they didn't call one. That's what a high school ref thinks playing through it means.

I'll take this time to say that while you are currently mad at NBA rules, they are designed to prevent exactly this. Yes, I could make ANYTHING look like an accident by the end of my career. ANYTHING. Even that thing that you're thinking 'there's no way you can make that look natural.' That, too. Especially that. I digress.

Will Peddy did not charge after me to fight, because he was looking for the bottom half of his front tooth. He was scrambling around on the ground until he found it. The play had been stopped, so when he did finally locate the tooth, he had time to stand up and look me directly in the eye, bloody mouth and all, while they walked him off the floor.

I'm unsure what prompted this, because I never did this before, but when he looked at me, all I could think to do was wink.

FUCKKKKK YOUUUUUU.

We won the game and I looked good doing it. I had won the war against overgrown football players in high school basketball, forever. Or so I thought.

Two years later, I was with my boy Alex. Alex was on my AAU and high school teams, and had since enrolled at UCLA. He was always eager to get me out to the Wooden Center and run the court. This was the summer before my sophomore year, so I hadn't really matured as a player yet. Also, I still enjoyed playing at rec centers because it was the only place I could feel the dominance I was supposed to as a D1 player. So with that in mind and because Alex and his 5'11" Jewish frame needed a ringer, we would get down often.

One day a couple football players, including Marcedes Lewis, walked in while we were playing. Lewis was a highly rated high school power forward and had since ditched basketball to become a star tight end on the UCLA football team. It was like my worst nightmare walked in. A football player who was also actually good at basketball? I knew it was going to be a long day.

That was when Will Peddy walked in and started warming up. I realized nobody knows their worst fears until they see them, cause there it was and it was getting worse. The two joined three other football slash basketball guys and lined up against myself, Alex, and three members of the Jewish fraternity, A E Pi. This was going to get ugly.

All the Jewish kids looked at me like I was going to save us — after all, I was the only actual basketball player there. But I was looking at each of them to help save me. Each of them seemed so large just minutes before when we were playing ZBT, but now looked so small, frail, and un-athletic next to a started NCAA offensive line.

It was the first day I really wished Alex wasn't Jewish. I wished I was on a team of Omega Psi Phi's instead of AePi's. We needed muscle and melanin, but we were going to find none here. Alas, Alex, Avi, someone they called "RENOB," and a kid in a Kippah lined up to play the actual Monstars.

It was brutal from the jump. Honestly, the game did go exactly like the Toon Squad vs the Monstars, except there was no Secret Stuff. I just got the shit kicked out of me, basically. It wasn't in a fighting sense, but in a 'if I call this foul this will turn into a fight' type of way. And with that, I called almost no fouls.

Honestly, I'm unsure if Peddy even remembered me. I don't think we spoke. But I really think he did. In my mind, he got word that the dude who broke his face and winked at him was running open gym in the wrong city, so he grabbed his boys and came down to give me the ass kicking I deserved.

Or maybe they don't even remember at all. Wild shit like that was college.

ZERO DEGREES

I was posted in San Francisco towards the end of summer 2008 while waiting for my agent to lock down a deal. That deal, which came seemingly out of nowhere, landed me in France. One day I was at the world's biggest pillow fight near Pier 33, and the very next day I was on an Air France flight to CDG. I had gotten used to life coming at me fast.

I was excited to play in France. I really was. I visited when I was 15, bought cologne for the first time, and visited the Eiffel tower. As I sat on a boat touring the river, I could see myself finding a wife out there. To me, it was the epitome of Romance. That was a lie.

When I actually arrived in Nancy, France, I wasn't really mad at it. It was clean, the town square looked like Marseille, and the team was a contender. There were great food options and some decent bars. As a basketball player, that's really all I could ask for. It was also near Luxemburg, which I decided I definitely needed to visit. There was only one issue in those first few days: they gave me a stick shift vehicle. Let me rephrase that: they gave me a Peugeot 206.

The Peugeot is not a bad car, frankly speaking. I'm unsure if they make sedans, but in those days, all I ever saw were hatchbacks. So, no matter what, a hatchback was my only option I knew. If they did make other models, for the life of me I don't understand why those weren't given to the basketball players.

That said, the car models were actually very neatly organized by number. The 200s were the smallest by size, and the 400's were pretty big. The third number described the engine size and luxury level. So, for example, my best friend on the team, Lamayne Wilson, had a jet black 307. That shit was smooth man. Paint was on point. Engine purred. Radio slapped.

Back to my shit: I had an overcast gray 206. It was so small that I had to turn backwards to get in. The radio sounded worse than my Logitech iPod dock, which I routinely brought into the car with me for that very reason. The engine sounded like a kazoo. It had one digital display on the whole car and it displayed the weather in celsius, often just reading "0." That weather reading would never be necessary, though, because it was cold as balls as I walked past the cemetery every morning to fire the 206 up. Annnnd, worst of all, it was a motherfucking stick shift.

Before I knew all that, I asked them for a different car.

"Why?"

So French.

"It's too small and I can't drive a stick shift. At all," I said, thinking my logic was undeniable. "Can I just get the same car everyone else has?"

"Not possible," he said blankly.

I didn't know it at the time, but before I left France I would hear that phrase 27,898 more times.

The next day it was time to learn how to drive this car at 8am before 10am practice. I had been able to get the car home so easily, it seemed maybe I had already figured it out. I hadn't. I failed to realize that driving a stick shift downhill wasn't really driving, it was gliding down the hill. I wasn't flying. I was falling with style.

That morning I had to go up a two mile long hill, complete with 10 stop lights, leading directly to the arena. It was zero degrees out and I was in a full sweat. I googled a tutorial, but there wasn't a lot out there.

Stick shifts, it seems, fell into an internet category of 'if you're googling this, welcome to a page that laughs at you.' My confidence was not high.

I got the car to move in first gear. I figured that would be enough to get me to practice, and it might have been, except I hit the first light and had to stop. Of course three cars pulled up right behind me, even though the street had two full lanes on each side.

These dudes better go around.

When the light turned green, I tried to shift into gear and the whole shit just turned off and started rolling backward. I panic slammed every lever and pedal available and thank baby Jesus it stopped. I had come within inches of hitting the nice 308 right behind me. I bet it was self-driving it was so nice.

It was then that the cars behind me figured out that I was out-classed in the 206 and that they should go around. I tried again. After twenty feet of rollback, I got it into first gear. Back up the hill and directly into the next light. Two cars pulled up directly behind me again.

AYO YALL ARE FUCKING ME RIGHT NOW!

This time, I didn't even try. The car behind me was too close. They also didn't move. They just sat there honking. It was such a French ass thing to do. All they had to do was go around, but instead they sat there honking until the light turned red again.

This whole process essentially repeated 10 times for all 10 lights. By the time I crossed the 10th light, not only was I late for my 10am practice, but my internal dialogue had changed. I no longer wanted anyone to go around when they pulled up behind me. I just let us all suffer.

Not possible, bitch.

It only took two days in France for me to realize it was ass.

EMAILS FROM BILL 2

From: BILL

To:???

Sent: 9/4/2008 9:45:01 A.M. Eastern Daylight Time

Subj: Re: Character

No offense to ————, who is hugely talented, but Rod is a hugely talented writer. How do I tell him to stop writing? He is going to end up on Saturday Night Live as a comedy writer. Keep up your good work. Listen, when I read it, I thought, 'oh crap, I hope — is not involved.' Thanks.

In a message dated 9/4/2008 9:40:38 A.M. Eastern Daylight Time,

??? writes:

As it is, they cut --- (but of course not before giving him $100,000.) I do think they were blindsided by this --- stuff. As for ---, believe me, they were very scared, which is why they were waffling. And, yes, -- did mention to me how they were not happy, at all, with ---- video blogs for ESPN and basically told him to immediately desist. Freedom of speech ends at Biscayne Boulevard.

From: BILL

Sent: Thu 9/4/2008 9:08 AM

To:-------

Subject: Character

--: I just thought you would be amused by this. When I brought ------ in to visit, ---- kept bombarding him/me about questions of character, past, on and on. When I brought Rod Benson in and he apparently destroyed --------, they brought up his blog. This is not to suggest ---- has a negative character because he used marijuana, if he used it, but you see what you want to see in a ------- or --------, that is, if you have more talent, some questions probably do not get asked. I did get a chuckle, however, as they emphasized this crap more than others. And Rod Benson is just a funny guy whose character is beyond reproach...he "just does not fit our team," I was told. Why? Because he thinks for himself and would rather write stupid, nonsensical stuff about North Dakota women than sit in a room with girls whose names you do not know and smoke dope. OK. I buy that!

Bill Neff

MILK CARTON

Whenever I was with my AAU team, everything was always so unpredictable. One could say we had a 'Bad News Bears' - ness to us. Someone was ALWAYS in some shit. But it wasn't big shit. We just always found new and interesting ways to upset the whole group.

There is no smaller example or one that sent everyone into a greater frenzy than when, before playing his team, one of my teammates got Tyson Chandler's autograph.

Oh man. Oh, oh man. The way the guys tore this kid a new one, mostly with jokes about his manhood, for DAYS. Mind you, this was before KD joined a 73 win team. No one understood at all whatsoever why this man would want a competitor's autograph. No one was that buddy-buddy.

I'm unsure if he was kicked off the team or he never came back, but that man and his autograph were never heard from again. I hope he found peace.

FIGUEROA

In the Spring of 2003, the Cal basketball team was in Los Angeles for the Pac 10 Tournament. As part of the festivities, there was a Pac 10 Hall of Honor event celebrating Kareem Adbul Jabbar as the inaugural inductee. All the teams in the league were there for the hours-long ceremony, split into tables of eight or so.

I noticed that there were eight small white basketballs on each table in front of us. Where I come from, a white basketball is for signing, not dribbling. So I grabbed one of the balls and looked around the room.

No outsiders were allowed in so there was no one who I could sign the ball for. No children were nearby to delight in the signature of a guy they didn't know. I couldn't sign one for my teammates, but unless it was a joke.

Could be funny.

I could get someone's autograph, but in a room full of peers, that seemed crazy. Who would forgive me for getting Salim Stoudemire to sign a ball? No one but a Wildcat or a fan of an extremely wet jumper.

It was then that it clicked that the balls must be for Kareem to sign. He was one of the two greatest players ever (LeBron had yet to play), famous, the ceremony was for him, and no one else there was worth an autograph. It made perfect sense. I decided I needed to ask him to sign my ball when the ceremony was over. I told my nearby teammates what my plan was.

"Nigga yes," is what David Paris answered when I asked if he wanted to get Kareem's autograph as well.

In the end, four or five of us waited patiently for Kareem to finish his acceptance speech, which was not a quick one. Finally he was done and the banquet was over. I started to get up quickly in case he got taken away before I could get to him. This turned out to be a good idea because as soon as he finished his speech, like the second he stopped talking, he took off walking. FAST.

Kareem is a few inches taller than me, and in 2003 he was still very spry. I say this because as we tried to walk after him, his pace was so fast that we had to jog to catch him. When I finally got to him, I asked him if he could sign the ball and he didn't say a word. He didn't break stride. He didn't even look at me. It was then that I heard someone say "I'll handle that for you."

I realized there was a small white man running alongside us.

"Hi. Yes a bit of an unusual situation. Why don't you hand me the balls and I'll coordinate with Mr Jabbar," he said as his tie flapped in the downstream of Kareems stride.

We literally exchanged the balls while jogging through the downtown LA Marriott lobby while Kareem kept walking. After he got the balls, the white man was now struggling to run, navigate the multiple escalators, but he persisted.

We kept jogging alongside him, and he was a few paces behind Kareem who had not once paused. Bro I'm not even sure Kareem was breathing. You know those videos where like 100 Chinese people in suits walk past one another in a criss cross fashion? How their arms swing so high side to side? It was like that, and equally impressive because it was just one man doing it somehow.

He walked right through the lobby and out the front door of the hotel and directly into the back of a limo. He left the door open and the man jumped in with the balls. My teammates and I stopped and looked at one another as the limo door shut and the car began to drive away. We hadn't had time to catch our breath but our eyes met.

How is Kareem Abdul Jabbar in better shape than me?

Out of nowhere, the window of the limo opened and the balls came flying out all at once, bouncing down the slope of the driveway alongside the moving car and into traffic on Figueroa. We ran out and negotiated traffic until we had grabbed all five balls. They had all been signed.

My mom has had that ball in a case in her office for twenty years. I never told her how I got it.

OWN THAT SHIT.

Have you been blessed with more money than you know what to do with?

How many button up shirts do you own that are exclusively for parties?

If the answer is over "zero," you can own a basketball franchise!

You'll get to hang around with cool black people all the time, travel to Scottsdale twice a year, and, if you're lucky, you can avoid scandal and keep the team forever!

BUT! Scandal or not, when you're ready, you can sell for billions! Win-win-win!

DD
DIFFERENT DUDE™

GAME WINNERS
AND SHIT

In the summer of 2012, I was starting to really feel myself. With all the money I made, the party had to keep getting bigger and bigger and 2012 was probably the peak of this expansion. This was the year I finally made it into the Playboy mansion (thanks to Josiah Johnson sneaking me in). I was living in a penthouse loft. I was pushing the AMG Mercedes. This was peak 'Rod Benson.'

An impromptu Vegas trip was standard fare back then. The BOOMTHO movement was in full effect, so each trip to Sin City was a huge branding opportunity. We'd bring all sorts of gear, slap bracelets, mascots, and boom boxes (super necessary before 2009).

My boy JMills and I drove into Vegas on some random shit on June 7, 2012. I know the date because as I write this, Facebook memories showed me photos from that day. We got into town and stayed at the Tropicana. It was a weird choice, but I wanted to get their most expensive room just to see how far my dollar could go. So I got some super fancy, super cheap room. We were ready to rock.

Day one, we found out that Calvin Harris was going to DJ at Encore Beach Club (EBC), so that was the play. I told the homegirl Celina to meet us there and she was hyped.

"OMG. I didn't know you liked Calvin!"

"I really don't even know what he looks like, but it's the summer of 2012 and we all know Calvin Harris is a big deal."

I didn't really say it like that, but that doesn't make it any less true. I didn't know who he was or what he looked like, but Calvin Harris was as unavoidable as the Kardashians. I knew the song 'Feel So Close,' but that was really all I knew of him or EDM in general. 2012 was the year that casuals like me were forced to learn EDM forever, and Calvin Harris was essentially the 101 class of the genre.

Because I didn't know what he looked like, a running joke started. I had all these random people at my table, smashing bottles of Stoli Elit vodka, and every time the DJ changed I'd jump up and start going wild, only to have Celina look up at me and laugh out the words "that's not Calvin."

After three or four rounds of this, Calvin finally took the stage. I was so lit that I hardly remembered what he looked like in the end. But it was a very fun $4000 experience.

When the party ended, JMillz, Celina and I were walking out laughing, clearly still in party mode. I was walking and talking, when some dude just walked right into my chest.

"Watch where the fuck you're going," he said plainly.

"Watch where the fuck *you're* going," I said back as I kept walking.

Within half a second, I was in handcuffs and thrown up against a cop car. I hadn't even seen police or cars and now they were all I could see and feel. JMillz was thrown against the car, too. Celina was not taken. Maybe she was a step behind us?

"Hey what is this?!" I screamed and pleaded. It all happened so fast.

"Shut the fuck up," the officer yelled back.

Why is any of this happening?

"This is bullshit," I said, hoping someone would see this and stop the madness. There were hundreds of people around.

"What?" The officer asked, in challenge.

"This is bullshit."

They threw JMillz and me into the back of a car that I did not fit in AT ALL. My legs were up against the door and roof of the car, over JMillz body, and my hands were pinned beneath me. Handcuffed, the pressure caused my right hand to go numb in seconds, and it stayed numb the entire ride to the local jail. They booked us and threw us in.

All of this was wild, but it only dawned on me that JMillz hadn't said a single fucking word this whole time when he offered some advice:

"We're here early. Grab the toilet paper. It's going to make a good pillow. We're going to be here a while."

"This is super fucked up, right?" I asked him, looking for reassurance.

"Yea. I didn't do shit," he said.

Neither of us should be in jail, but Millz had literally done nothing.

"I think I get the black thing now, man," he continued. "That *was* super fucked up."

Did I mention JMillz is white?

I grabbed the TP and laid down on it. We had been partying all day, and it was only really starting to hit me. We had finished off the bottles right at the end of the party, with plans to go party some more, not go directly to jail and not collect $200. Millz was right, though. Not only was the TP a great pillow, but a couple hours later, everyone wanted it. The whole room was full of unsavory folks.

They let us go at 5:00 am. I couldn't believe how mentally scarring it was to be locked up, even for twelve hours. As soon as I was free, I knew that even one minute of future jail would be my undoing.

I checked my phone and I had a hundred missed messages, mostly from Celina who was confused and scared. There were also hella messages from women I met that day, either thanking me for the hype or wanting to get together. All of it was a waste. I also had a pounding headache because there was not enough water coming from the toilet water fountain combo to offset how much alcohol we had.

After a few hours of sleep at the Tropicana, we decided to go even harder the next day to make up for the waste of the day before. Very 27 year-old logic. We went to Marquee to try to forget all our sorrows, and almost as soon as we walked in, some dude walked up to me and started talking.

"Bro that was fucked up yesterday. My Bad."

It was the guy who had bumped into me the day before.

"Man, that wasn't even on you," I shouted back over the music.

He explained that not only was he in a bad mood and looking to start shit, he didn't want it with me at all due to my size. When he saw me he knew he messed up, that's why he walked away. Further, he was shocked that the police didn't even look in his direction. I didn't even think about that. Dude, who is not black, just walked away from the ordeal while I went to jail.

I can hear you right now saying, "Rod, this is cool and a little sad, but why is this story in this book?"

I'll tell you why, because my numb right hand didn't go away. When mid July hit and I still couldn't feel my hand, I got worried. When August hit and it was time to go start camp, I panicked. When we were getting taped up before the opening night of the season and I had no feeling in my right hand, I realized the season could be doomed.

That first game I had something like 27 and 18 with no feeling in my shooting hand. As the season went on, I learned to play around it. I was slightly worse percentage-wise from the field, but to my knowledge, nobody knew that I played that entire season with a numb hand. We even won the championship, where I had game winners and shit. All of that was with no feelin'.

I thought my hand might be numb forever, but one day in the summer of 2013, the feeling just came back. I really don't think my touch was ever the same again, though. I had spent a whole season playing numb, my game was always off after that.

The Clark County Sheriff's office never even filed paperwork.

YOU DON'T GET IT

I find it odd how mature we are expected to be so young. Growing up, there were so many times we were asked questions way bigger than our understanding.

There was the time in fourth grade where I was asked if I was a virgin and I said no, then yes, then I don't know. All three were funny answers to other fourth graders. Why was I ever expected to know that?

In college, there were still large understandings we had yet to learn, and yet we were still hammered for that lack of knowledge or growth. At that age, religion was a huge pain point for people. Most college kids came from suburbs where most of the town they grew up in either believed the same religion, or had decided to not discuss it publicly like many parents of 90s kids. So when these kids got to college, it was the first time that what they learned in the home was tested by a wide audience.

This used to really fascinate me. I was struggling with growing up Christian myself, trying to navigate how much of it I believed and how much of it scared me. I tried to take cues from others. This was easy, because every single dude on the team was also Christian. In fact, in all my days playing hoops, probably 95% of my teammates were Christian. I assume it has something to do with being black and born in the 80s, but the numbers were staggering. I didn't have to do much to learn from others on the topic, because dudes would offer up their exact feelings all the time.

As it was, the one topic that came up the most was that of homosexuality. I can't tell you how many times I heard someone tell someone else that gay people were going directly to hell. Whether they said it nice or they said it mean or they said it flippantly and without emotion, they said it often.

A few of my teammates harbored those feelings. If you're finding that off putting, I ask that you don't, because this was not a source of comfort for these people. It was both fear of being called gay, which we all were, and fear that if they denounced one part of their religion they may have to denounce more of it, more of themselves, maybe even of their family. These were enormous questions for kids who were still getting their burritos paid for by their God fearing father.

One day, we found some Facebook photos of a teammate's brother. He didn't post the caption "I'm gay," but it was clear that the young man was now living in his truth. Instead of feeling joy for him, we saw this as a means to get my teammate to look foolish.

"What do you think of this picture?" Someone asked him in a bit of 'gotcha' friendship.

He studied the picture.

"I don't feel anything. Why are you showing me this?"

"That's your brother, right?"

"Yea. So what?"

"Nigga he gay."

"No he isn't."

I didn't understand how he could look at the picture and not make the same conclusion we all did. But I could see the torment on his face. He was struggling with the moment and being forced to confront a lot of feelings right in front of us. It was super fucked up. It got worse.

"Don't you think that all gay people go to hell?"

"Yes. They do," he replied sharply, "but my brother ain't gay. Shut the fuck up before I throw hands."

We never discussed it again. It seemed, in that moment, that we all finally found a little empathy for someone coping with new understanding for the first time.

It wasn't long after that his brother came out and everyone I knew, including my tormented teammate, supported him. I say that to say, we could have judged him on that moment forever, but I remember so vividly how much it hurt him to confront himself, then to grow, then to change. It was the first time I watched someone fully reject what they had been taught and the process wasn't fun.

THE PANIC BUTTON

My first season in North Dakota was wild for many reasons. One of the wilder things was moving into a city with a minuscule dating pool. We didn't realize how big the area of effect we had as just ten guys.

See, in a normal world, ten people don't disrupt shit. But in a town with 30k people, ten alpha males can do a lot of work because there really just aren't enough people to offset the sheer numbers of women some of these guys are used to meeting.

I'll save some of the specifics for other stories, but guys were out here hooking up with wives, flying women in, all sorts of stuff. I kept it easy (or so I thought) and dated a cheerleader, who they kicked off the team for dating me. I didn't think it was a big deal, so I did it again the next year with a different cheerleader and she was kicked off as well. It was all dumb.

Still, there were only a handful of women who were available and not on a banned book list or anything, and they were widely known among the team because the same couple guys had been casually hooking up with them for years. I remember one woman, I'll call her Tiff, was at our apartment complex three nights in a row to visit three different guys on the team and they all knew. This was not uncommon.

By my second year, I knew all these caveats and oddities about playing out there, but the new rookies had no idea. I'm not gonna lie, this led to some of the funniest experiences of my lifetime. I'm unsure what we knew or learned the previous year, but the new class missed all the memos and were in constant conflict with the vets. This wasn't just dating related. It got bad at times.

One of those rookies, Earnest, really struggled with all of that. He was a good kid, but situations always befell him. There was the time we were in a playoff game and he got upset at me (probably with good reason) and threw a chair at me. There was the time someone mentioned that he tends to "hit the panic button" when things go wrong, prompting him to frantically "search" the van for the "panic button" which then continued when we got back to the apartment for twenty more minutes. He really went through everyone's cabinets screaming "IS THE PANIC BUTTON IN HERE? IS IT?!"

Let's just say that Earnest was still figuring it out at that time in his life.

That's not to say that everyone wasn't rooting for him, because we were. Especially with the ladies. It's hard enough to meet someone, but it's even harder when you're shrouded in 6'9" dudes with unlimited confidence. In a city with slim pickens', it seemed like he was on the outside looking in often. I'm unsure if that's true, but it's something I think we all felt.

We all lived in one, six unit apartment building, two to an apartment. Earnest lived with Benjamin in one of the bottom floor units. I lived with Kibwe in the other one.

One night, I heard the unmistakable sounds of hardcore love making coming through the wall we shared. Earnest was in there GETTING IT. It was late by ND standards, maybe 1 a.m., and I was ready to call the authorities because it sounded like a murder was happening next door. The only reason I didn't was because every fourth word was "yes!"

I was just putting headphones on to go to bed when I was re-awoken by a loud "FUCK YOU!"

I jumped up and ran to the window. Drama happened often back then, and I was into it every single damn time.

The words were followed by loud banging on the bedroom window next to mine. I could see one of my vet teammates, Mike, in front of Earnest's window watching him have sex while banging on his window, cursing him out, trying to get him to stop. I can't tell you how much joy this filled me with. I kinda feel bad about it, but oh man did I smile watching tea spill so violently.

I guess 'what had happened was,' Earnest had gone out to the bar that night and met one of those few available women, who shot her shot. Earnest, being new to the old system, had no idea that the three man rotation she had been working with for years was already solid. That's right. Earnest was smashing Tiff, everyone could hear it, and the three guys who had a monopoly on her (whatever that meant) were not happy. Least of all, Mike.

I had totally forgotten that Mike and Tiff had history, but here I was, face glued to my bedroom window watching him beat on Earnest's window in the middle of the night, screaming "fuck you!" at both of them.

The very best part was that neither Tiff nor Earnest cared about the noise, the banging, or the cussing even one iota. They continued doing what I can only describe having heard it, as a remarkably tight rendition of when Simba and Nala realized they had parts, fully disregarding Mike in the process.

I secretly cheered this on. Not because I had a vendetta against Mike or anything, but because it felt like Earnest was fucking for his own respect. I'm not going to say for sure that he got it, but he can forever say he took the magic number from 3 to 4 and shook up the old ways.

He hit a lot more than the panic button.

17 AGAIN

I was finally starting to feel like an adult after my first season out of college. I had made *some* money, I lived in an apartment, my friend groups were beginning to shift. Everything was starting to feel alright. I took that plucky attitude into an H&R Block. Adults pay taxes, right?

"We have some great news! And some not so great news!"

The green shirted dude was yelling. I had never heard great/not-great before, so I didn't know where to place my fear.

"At your income level, you'll be getting our cheapest rate! And... Wait... You qualify for the 'round the block' deal! Half off!"

I might be making up that name of the deal, but it was something like that.

Nothing bad whatsoever...

"So, what's not so great?" I asked while scanning the round the block deal paperwork.

"So like I said, because of our promotion, you can file for $40! Isn't that cool?"

The guy had me hyped.

"Hell yea! Lets get it!"

"Great! So $40, filed 17 times... The total today will be $680. Simple!"

"Naww player. I... That doesn't add up," I said with the crackled voice of an adolescent. I was also now laying on the floor. Did I pass out?

The guy explained that I had technically earned my money in 16 states, so I had to file all 16 and federal, even though I made a total of $4200 pre tax, and had $1800 of that taken out before I ever got it. So I was getting nothing back, and had to pay H&R Block $680 just to file.

My adulthood ended that day. I didn't pay taxes for years after that. It all caught up to me, too.

NEVER FORGIVE ME

One thing people really don't get is that all basketball players play games on Christmas, so they kind of don't have a Christmas. I don't care if it's pro or High school, there are games on or near Christmas, often requiring travel. So basically the day I made varsity in high school, I lost Christmas for 20 years.

My mom was not happy. Not only was I always in the middle of season and unable to go home, I had to constantly remind people I wouldn't even really be available for calls and whatever either.

When I was in the D-League, in my second season, we played a Christmas day game in Des Moines. I remember it was weird, not just because of the game and the fact that a town like Des Moines FULLY shuts down on Christmas, but also because Obama was in town to give a campaign speech. So the streets were both emptier than normal and also randomly open for Obama stuff.

I don't remember if we won or lost, but I remember after the game, people were trying to get active in the streets. Compared to Bismarck, North Dakota where we lived, Des Moines may as well have been Miami. No matter that it was Christmas, snowing, and Obama was in town, there *had* to be some sort of bar open.

I could have gone either way. I was going to drink, for sure, but beyond that it seemed there wasn't a lot to do. That's when my teammates started suggesting we find a strip club.

This happened all the time. In fact, thinking back, there were probably more nights that began with someone suggesting a strippy than anything else. Not being a fan, I would always push back. Why the hell would everyone ALWAYS want to go to strip clubs?

No one ever cared about my dissenting opinion. Ever. As a result, I've been to strip clubs everywhere from Albuquerque to Poland (the country). Hoopers just love suggesting the coddamn strip club right off top.

Back to Christmas night, the strip club chorus was getting louder. All the restaurants and bars were fully closed or encased in some Obama shit, so if a strip club was available, guys were gonna be down to go.

We didn't have google maps like that and, even if we did, strip clubs weren't exactly indexed in those days so I'm unsure how we even inquired. I think someone asked the front desk or a taxi driver or something, because we definitely found one.

I found myself in this position often. I'm in a small town, middle of nowhere, 10 teammates all into doing something, and myself really having to choose between doing the thing or kicking it alone at the hotel. For 20 years, this was always the choice: hotel alone or something random with the squad. On Christmas night, I did not desire to be alone, so I got in the taxi with the team and we were off to find some nude Iowans.

We drove for SO LONG. Maybe an hour. I don't mean a Los Angeles hour, either. In Iowa, with empty streets and highways fully open, an hour might have gotten us to Canada. So I really don't know where we ended up – in part because it was so dark and in part because we drove so long. There were no street lights the further we got out of the city, so all I could see were the corn fields lit up by the headlights of the taxi. I felt like we were driving into a chainsaw massacre.

Out of nowhere, some lights of a place I'm pretty sure was a converted Pizza Hut came into view. I wish I could remember the name, but it just kind of appeared almost like a mirage. It was just corn, and then, a strip club.

The driver then turned into a corn lined driveway that had to be a mile long itself and creeped over the bumpy dirt road. Chainsaw massacre shit.

IF I DIE OUTSIDE A DES MOINES STRIP CLUB ON CHRISTMAS THE STREETS WILL NEVER FORGIVE ME

We got out of our taxis and walked in. There were no patrons at all, save for us. A rather unappealing lady was working the pole, sadly. It then hit me that the strippers were stripping on Christmas. It was both sad and funny. The fact that they were there working the chainsaw shift on Christmas night was sad. The fact that we as patrons were clearly watching the best this club could scrap together was funny.

We went to grab some beers, but they didn't sell liquor. Having been to so many clubs by now, I can say that strip clubs always have weird rules depending on the state. Vegas has no rules. Boise they can't get nude so they wear bathing suits. Iowa they can't get nude and sell alcohol at the same time. We knew exactly what this was when they didn't sell beer.

Upon realizing we would have to watch two B-team strippers, sober, on Christmas, we ran back out before the taxis could leave. We weren't going to wait another hour in a haunted strip club.

I woke up the next day and watched Obama give his speech. It could have focused more on the local economy if you ask me.

THE OPS.

How much do you love basketball? A lot? Like, a lot a lot?

Do you have any contacts in the sport? No? None at all?

That's OK!

The world of basketball operations awaits! All you need to do is show up and start working, and soon enough (but never soon enough), you'll start really enjoying having a title nobody can define!

That's OK!

The first time an NBA player pays you $100 to eat something dumb, you'll feel a part of the team.

DD
DIFFERENT
DUDE™

KFC

When I got to North Dakota, it was my first time ever joining a team without doing camp or anything like that. One day I was in LA, the next day I was in Bismarck. There was a lot I was not prepared for, including the crippling sickness I contracted upon landing in -20 degree weather with a hoodie on.

There seemed to be many secrets to living a good life out there. Whereas I was always broke, tired, cold, and hungry, my teammates appeared to be none of the above. How? We made the same amount of money. Had they earned some money overseas and brought it back? It couldn't have been all of them.

One day I saw some of my teammates absolutely destroying some KFC. These negroes had to be broke like me. How was this possible?

"Nigga ask Tom," was the only response anyone would give me.

I guess I should ask Tom.

Tom Waggoner and Mike Offerdahl ran the ops out in North Dakota. They were probably the first ops guys I got to know well in my career. Their job was to do a million jobs. They got jerseys for us, produced games, handled media requests and paychecks, and most importantly to me at the time, Tom handled gift certificates.

I didn't know this until we spoke. It felt kind of like I was going in to meet Tony Montana or something. He could not have been more kind, but my mind was gripped with fear. 'Nigga ask Tom' wasn't the most reassuring messaging. But here I was face to face with Tom, the dream maker.

"How many?" He asked without lifting his eyes from his screen. Boss shit.

"Umm I... Uh. Two?"

He slid me two gift certificates to KFC.

"Next time you'll have to earn 'em," he mentioned as I walked out.

I ATE SO MUCH KFC THAT NIGHT. MOTHERFUCKING SHIT I ATE LIKE A KING. I TRIED TO RATION MY TWO GIFT CARDS BUT I ABSOLUTELY COULD NOT.

It was only a week later and I was desperate again. This time Tom had me where he wanted me.

"From here on out if you want these, you're going to have to do appearances around town. Each appearance is a gift certificate. You get it?"

"Shit I get it. Sign me up."

It was like the movie "Casino." The Colonel, who I never met, would give the certificates to Tom, at a rate that was never shared with me. Plausible deniability was important for the operation. Tom had the supply, and therefore the power. If something needed attending, the city would have to go through him.

I became the guy who could get you things. I...

I'm getting confused. All I know is I did so many appearances it was stupid. Got some school kids? I'm there. Walmart opening? Let's rock. Carpet Emporium needs bodies? SIGN ME UP. I was everywhere.

I remember one day I was at Gold's Gym for an appearance and not a single person showed up. It was just me, a pen, and hella game schedules. Not a soul wanted one. I would have been upset, but those eleven herbs and spices were on my mind.

By season's end, I had figured out the system. It was actually a good one, because I got to meet and interact with damn near everyone in town. I was more tapped in than anyone.

People always ask how much I hated living in North Dakota, and I always tell them it wasn't as bad as they might think.

"How the hell can it not be that bad?" they ask.

"I don't think you realize Bismarck got a KFC," I reply.

EMAILS FROM BILL 3

From: Some Guy with Orlando

To: BILL

Sent: 3/26/2008 2:27:29 P.M. Eastern Daylight Time

Subj: RE: Rod Benson

Bill,

Nobody does it better than you.

This is good stuff.

To follow up on our earlier conversation......we definitely have interest in Rod. We'll talk at a later date.

-SGWO

. . .

From: BILL

Sent: Wed 3/19/2008 4:13 PM

To: ---@utahjazz.com; ---@utahjazz.com; --@hor-
nets.com;-----@pacers.com; ---@blazers.com; ---
@washsports.com; ---@washsports.com; ---@celtic-
s.com; ---@dallasmavs.com; ---@dallasmavs.com; --
-@clippers.com; ---@la-lakers.com; ---@la-laker-
s.com; ---@kingsbball.com; ---@kingsbball.com; --
-@kingsbball.com; -----@gs-warriors.com; ---@sun-
s.com; ---@njnets.com;; ---@bobcatsbasketball.-
com; ---@bulls.com; j---@palacenet.com;-----
@palacenet.com; ---@pacers.com; ---@grizzlies.-
com; ---@heat.com; ---@heat.com;-----@milwaukee-
bucks.com; ---@timberwolves.com; ---
@thegarden.com; --@clippers.com;-----@celtics.-
com; ---@cavs.com;-----@utahjazz.com;-----@pepsi-
center.com; --@timberwolves.com; ---
@atlantaspirit.com;------@torontoraptors.com; ---
-@clippers.com; ---@pepsicenter.com; ---@bulls.-
com; ----@attcenter.com; ---@attcenter.com; ---
@sixers.com; ----@torontoraptors.com; ----@wash-
sports.com; ---@atlantaspirit.com; ---@timber-
wolves.com;----@njnets.com; ---
@bobcatsbasketball.com; -----@bobcatsbasketball.-
com; -----@bulls.com;-------@clippers.com; ----
@heat.com; -----@bobcatsbasketball.com; ------
@blazers.com;------@suns.com; ----@kingsbball.-
com; --@cavs.com; -----@cavs.com; -----
@atlantaspirit.com; ----@palace.net; ------@griz-
zlies.com; ----@Sonics-Storm.com; ----@Sonics-
Storm.com; ---@thegarden.com; ----@njnets.com; --
---@attcenter.com; ----@rocketball.com; ----@com-
cast-spectacor.com; ----@grizzlies.com; ----
@rocketbball.com; ------@thegarden.com;------

126

@bellsouth.net; —--@rocketball.com; —-@rocketbal-l.com; —----@gs-warriors.com; —---@comcast-spec-tacor.com; —----@njnets.com

Subject: Rod Benson

Gentlemen: Consider these numbers for the NBDL's Rod Benson, please:

--Statistically, he is the 3rd best rebounder/minute in professional basketball in the US, playing for Dakota

Name Rebounding Average/Game Rebounds/Minute

D. Howard 13.7 2.56

Camby 14.4 2.68

Benson 12.2 2.75

Chandler 12.3 2.85

Kaman 13.1 2.9

Jefferson 11.6 3.11

--He leads the NBDL by over 4 rebounds/game over the next closest pursuer while averaging 13 PPG

--His team is leading its Division even though it lost its two leading guards to Europe

--He has had 20 double doubles, tops in the NBDL

--Consider his numbers vs. these NBA players playing in the D League:

. . .

Name Rebounding Average/Game Rebounds/Minute

Benson 12.2 2.75

Fesenko 7.5 3.36

Samb 7.1 3.66

O'Bryant 9.5 3.79

Mahinmi 7.9 3.8

Simmons 6 4.8

--So, why is he still there? His weight? He outweighs Mikki Moore; he weighs the same as Marcus Camby

--His age? He is only 23 years old

--In the Championship game last year in the NBDL, he helped Dakota win with his five blocked shots

--Says one NBA assistant coach, "he picks up pick & roll schemes better than any player in the League"

--Says one veteran NBDL GM, "Rebounding is the one statistic which should translate to the next level"

Remember, how difficult it was for Mikki Moore to get called up. Then, he was called up, signed a three year deal and then had to endure a second minor league stint with Roanoke. Mikki only has had 64 starts this season for Sacramento!

Bill Neff

TO THE STREETS

"Do you want to go by the last name 'Kidd?'"

My mom seemed to think that age 9 was the first age I should have some agency over my name. I thought about it for a while, and decided that Rod Benson was a good enough name. It sounded like a good baseball player name like Ken Griffey or Frank Thomas. Rod Kidd had too many "D"s.

She made the offer after my grandfather, Clarence Kidd, came to visit and took us to the Grand Canyon. The trip, albeit fun, was hella confusing. I don't think I had met this grandfather prior to the trip and the name Kidd was new. I was Benson, my mom Holmes, her sisters all had different names. Last names were a weird thing in my family.

A few months later, Jason Kidd began to take the NBA by storm. The first guard to get triple doubles since Magic? I was instantly a fan.

I wanna be Kidd now.

Fast forward ten years and I'm about to start my freshman year at Cal. The decision had nothing to do with Jason, but the decision was still made. My mom told the coaches that I was related to Jason Kidd and the media team had to run with it. They asked me questions about him that I really didn't know the answer to. I told them we had never met, but the connection was through my grandfather in Shreveport. They loved the non-story and prominently displayed it in the media guide as a rad piece of Golden Bear trivia or something. I didn't want to make the story too big a deal, though, because I was trying to make my own name. Only the few folks who actually read the media guide ever knew.

Fast forward to 2007. I signed with the Nets for camp and headed out there the day after Memorial Day. I know that because on Memorial Day I was at White Party at Richard Jefferson's house where I told him we would be teammates in New Jersey. He gave me the nod of a dude who knew we wouldn't be teammates long. He was correct.

The first time I actually met Jason Kidd was at the practice facility in the middle of nowhere, New Jersey. The NBA media people were way more excited and aggressive about this information than they were at Cal. A media guy introduced me to Jason and forced us to chat about our relationship right away while he was getting taped up. Literally we had never spoken, and the first words out of his mouth were "really?"

"Uh.. yea," I said.

I lost all the confidence I had had for 15 years. I wanted some kind of warm up and I didn't get it.

"Who's the connection?"

"Clarence Kidd. My grandfather out of Shreveport."

"Oh ok. Well that's cool."

It was clear he didn't know who I was talking about, but I knew the connection so I didn't trip. Also, I didn't want to really talk about it in our first ever conversation so I let it die. I was cut from the Nets in mid October and I have never spoken to Jason since.

Fast Forward to 2017. I'm sitting in Korea when I get an email from my mom that read something like:

"Finally got info from your grandmother. Found out my real father is in Atlanta. Flying to Atlanta tomorrow. Will update soon."

Weird email, mom.

And with that email, I found out that in the 60's my grandmother essentially belonged to the streets, had many different… friends… and that I spent years lying about being cousins with Jason Kidd.

OH

Years after college, I was somewhere with Paul, a former star football player at Cal and some other friends. We weren't close in college, mainly because I really was immature and it took people a while to acclimate to my personality. But at that moment, we were all grown killers. He felt empowered to share.

"In college we thought you were on a special scholarship," he announced.

"What's that mean?"

"You know. *Special.*"

"Oh shit."

"I'd walk by the computer lab and you would be staring into the distance with your mouth open for so long, we all just thought you were... yea."

WHO IS WE?

HANGANG PARK

In mid August, 2010, I was drafted 6th in the Korean Basketball League draft. Two weeks later, instead of preparing for NBA training camp, I was on a flight to Incheon, South Korea. Two more weeks later and I was already looking for things that reminded me of home. It's odd, because at the time, I don't think I actively felt homesick, but looking back I certainly was.

One day, I saw a poster for a music festival called Global Gathering with Fatboy Slim headlining stapled to a wall. I wasn't some big Fatboy Slim fan, but in a new country where nothing made sense, seeing a familiar act felt important. I was also hoping to make some friends in Korea because at the time I had none and I figured some American Expats would be likely to attend. So random Korean EDM festival, it was.

I googled the location of the event, printed out the map, grabbed some drank for the ride, and jumped into a taxi. I showed the driver the printed out location and map and he made a surprised sounding noise (not uncommon) and began to drive.

As I sat in this car, I was basically just drinking in silence. That's because Korean taxis often don't play music and my US based iPhone didn't work out there. I didn't have internet, texting, or music streaming that worked at all. Not to mention that the driver spoke zero English, so I was sitting there with absolutely no distraction. It was a totally new situation.

After some time, I had been sitting in traffic in a taxi for over an hour. Only then did I realize something must have been wrong because the venue was supposed to only be 20 minutes away. An hour turned into an hour and a half and then to two hours and I just kept riding along quietly.

I wasn't speaking, reading, listening, connecting, or any other thing that could take me out of the moment. It may have been the first time I had ever been truly present. By that I don't mean focused, but present; living truly in the moment and feeling everything it entails. It felt dreadful. I felt the weight of existence for the first time and due to its weight, I broke down in tears. I sat in the back of this taxi and I sobbed.

The wild part is that to that point, I never ever cried. I would sit in a room full of people breaking down and feel bad that I couldn't get there. Even until recently I used to worry I wouldn't cry at my wedding or important funerals. I was not emotionally tapped in.

In that moment, though, it felt like all the emotion I had ever held in came rushing out. It was as if my entire life, the basketball, the blogging, the clothing, the girlfriend, were all overlays on top of a sadness that had never been addressed. It was uncomfortable. It hurt. It was both horrible and beautiful, my face in my hands trying not to make sniffling sounds.

The lesson I thought I learned that day was that I had unresolved trauma that was closer to the surface than I ever allowed myself to believe, and that may be true. But looking back, there are a couple other reasons for the breakdown.

First, I was finally overseas for the long haul and I was handling it well by suppressing the connected parts of myself. I used to pride myself on the fact that I didn't need to be on Skype all day or need family to travel with me, but that was a mask. Second, this was the first time I had ever truly detached from Western life and I had an identity crisis once there was no noise to distract me.

All of that culminated in one big understanding: I was alone. And if I wanted to be good at international basketball, I'd have to be good at being alone. In the moment, I chose to be good at basketball, and the overlays went back up.

I arrived at the concert eventually and had a decent time. I didn't even tell anyone about the taxi ride for years. But now when I describe what the weight of overseas basketball really is, the part that we athletes feel constantly but never contextualize, I tell the story of Hangang Park.

I'm thankful for the experience.

LINDALEE'S FEET

I'm unsure how it happened, but in the Spring of 2012 I ended up lightly talking to a women's basketball player from Pepperdine named Monica. I say I'm unsure how it happened, because I felt a little old for her. She was 21 or 22 and I was only 26, but I had traveled the world, juggled the brand, and lived in Korea and she was a college student. Nothing wrong with that, but mentally we were on some other stuff. She even once told me I was out of her league which I had never heard before.

When I got back from Korea, the boys and I headed out to Malibu on Easter Sunday. John mentioned that he wanted to go spend the day in Malibu to check in on his family friend, Lindalee.

Lindalee is the mother of one of John's oldest friends, Cameron. I had met all these people here and there, but I didn't really know them. It seemed like a lot to drop in on them on Easter Sunday, but John was steadfast. Keep in mind to make this move we had to turn down other options in LA, so he really had to sell this Malibu trip as something fun.

He was certain this would be the greatest day. I was less so. In my mind, unless you love spending thousands of dollars AND you want to do unnecessarily far away white things, Malibu isn't exactly a space I would call exciting.

In an effort to spice it up, I hit up Monica and asked if she was free that day. I could do a Sunday Funday and hang out with her for the first time, and that would be the event. She was both interested and available, so we made the plan. John and I would go by there, pregame, then meet Lindalee at the beach club for some white shit. It sounded good to all parties involved.

It was my brother, John, and I who headed out that day. When we got to Pepperdine, Monica was still getting ready. Her teammates were gonna get in on the action too, so we started taking shots while everyone was doing their thing. I'm unsure how many shots we took, but the three men in the room were all heavy hitters, and the women's basketball team ain't small. I feel like we finished a handle in about an hour, collectively. I was good. John was good. Chris was good.

We left to go to Lindalee's while everyone else was finishing up and they were going to meet us shortly. This is where everything went wrong. John, for whatever reason, did not take us to the beach club. In fact, Lindalee wasn't even there. She was at her very nice home. We walked up to the parking garage area, adjacent PCH.

"Man. We aren't going to the actual Easter brunch are we?"

I had to ask the obvious question.

"No man. No. it's not even like that. Run in right now. I'm gonna smoke this blunt," John responded. Gotta give it to the man, he lies with expert confidence.

It was then that Monica and a couple of the Pepperdine girls showed up. Monica was in a rush to get inside because she had to go to the bathroom. John repeated himself.

"I'm smoking. Lindalee is cool, man. Just go in."

We rushed up to the door because Monica signaled that there was some urgency. I rang the doorbell of this very nice and quiet home.

There was no answer. I tried again a minute later. Nothing. Monica looked at me like the clock was ticking so I walked back to John.

"Man. For real you gotta come over here. Lindalee ain't answering. Can you call her or something?"

"Bro! Oh my God, man. Stop knocking and go in!"

John was so adamant that he didn't have to do shit except smoke.

OK. I guess I'll just go in…

I headed back towards the house. It was a blind turn to go from the garage area to the front door. When I came around the corner, Lindalee was just cracking the door open and a wildly dancing Monica looked up at her frantically. As soon as the door got fully open, Monica pissed herself. It was a full out urination.

I never just watched a woman pee in the wild, let alone through a sundress, but it looked like she just had a bucket under there and turned it upside down. It was essentially just a gallon of water that appeared out of nowhere, splashing Lindalee's feet and getting on the porch. This whole ordeal took about a second and a half, which was enough time for me to take off running back to John without addressing any of it.

"John! It's all bad. We have to go. It's all bad!"

"What happened?!"

"We have to go. It's over. It's all over. Easter is ruined! We have to go now!"

"Rod! What the fuck are you saying?"

"She pissed," I was still catching my breath,"man, it's everywhere."

John took off towards Lindalee's door. No one was outside, but the rainwater was still there so he knew I wasn't lying. We went inside and Lindalee looked upset and confused. She thought we were coming over for Easter Dinner with the family, not a drunken Malibu Sunday Funday. On top of that, she had just been pissed on, and all she saw was me running away. Further, Monica was left there for Lindalee to deal with. Everything that could have been bad was bad.

"That poor girl is upstairs in the shower. I know it's not her fault."

No. It was my fault. I should never have trusted John. I shouldn't have dated out of my league. And I damn sure shouldn't have gone to Malibu expecting anything other than trouble.

CUT 2

"Are you a basketball player or are you a tourist?"

Jean-Luc Monschau put an extra french accent into the word 'tourist' in a way that made it sound like too-wist. I knew it was over when he asked that question as we sat at a sangria dinner HE SET UP.

I was cut from my French team the next day.

RE-CONDITIONING

With all the turmoil going on when I was in college, you'd think we were just out here without guidance. You'd be wrong. We had so much. Too much, maybe.

I question if it was too much because part of our support system was an in house sports psychologist, named Doc Carr. Assuming his first name isn't actually "Doc," all I ever knew about him really was that his last name was Carr, he was a doctor of something, and he had worked with Allen Iverson. Honestly, that was all he needed for credentials. I really did buy into what he was saying, early on at least.

As a freshman, Doc Carr was already a fixture of the team. I don't recall the day I met him or what he did with us at practice, but I damn sure remember the first team meeting with him.

"Ya'll don't say SHIT. Let us handle this whole meeting. If you get the Cake, give it to one of us," Brian Wethers told Richard, David and me right before our first Doc Carr meeting.

Cake? Oh hell yea..

There was no cake. 'Cake' was the term used for a basketball, and meant as a symbol. Whoever held the ball got to talk. It was a communication tool. I started to understand what was happening.

In the meeting, Brian and Joe basically just took turns with the Cake, responding to Doc Carr's hard hitting questions about our team chemistry and whatnot. They essentially shielded all of us from having to speak, which seemed to have two motivations. The first motivation was that they could keep us from saying something that would hurt ourselves or the team. This was our first rodeo, after all. The second thing was that they didn't want us bringing up some real shit that we had to untangle and stay hours longer than we needed to. It was a crash course in how to be a Senior.

These meetings happened sporadically going forward. The seniors handled them each time. I never said a word I didn't have to. It wasn't my place. The meetings were generally just something that felt annoying, but also part of the game. I did feel like we had some special advantage in being able to talk out issues, even if they were mundane.

Eventually I realized that most of the issues we talked about were bullshit. There was a lot of turmoil my sophomore year (some created by me) that all the Doc Carr shit didn't really help with. Whatever we said with Doc Carr felt empty compared to what we were actually dealing with. People liked talking about everything to their circles, but never to the group, and definitely not with the Cake in hand.

My Junior year this changed. We had no seniors, so myself, Richard, and David were the oldest on the team. It kind of snuck up on us. One day we were just some goofy sophomores, and the next day we had too much responsibility. Never mind that I was technically the same age as a couple of the freshmen, we were the ones that people looked up to. This was not a good idea, and Doc Carr helped us to understand why.

The first time we had a Doc Carr meeting my Junior year, he picked the topic right away. It was alcohol. All of us drank too much, myself near the top of the list. I never went out the night before games, but that was my own jiu jitsu justification. From the coaches perspective, David and I were out of control and, as leaders, that needed to change.

"When did you have your first drink of alcohol?"

Doc Carr asked as he threw me the Cake. I guess I was going to start.

"About 11 months ago," I replied.

The coaches looked shocked. I should also note that the coaches weren't always around for these meetings, but on this day they were. It was always a sign that there was something bigger at play.

"Is that true?" Doc Asked.

"It is," I said, still holding the cake.

I figure they expected me to give some long story about how I started at 15, had fully lost myself, and now I could use their help. Instead, they didn't get the satisfaction. That made me happy.

I passed the Cake to Richard. Doc repeated the question.

"Richard, when did you first drink?"

"I don't know. Twelve? Eleven?"

Richard's answer could not have been more perfect, especially after mine. Not only had this dude been drinking for a decade, he was teflon as far as the coaches were concerned, so they couldn't really check him on it. Plus he's British so on top of the funny accent delivery, when he announced that he was 12 when he started drinking, it kinda made sense. We all looked up at each other collectively.

Yeah that tracks.

Richard had ruined the whole game.

"Pass the Cake to David," Carr said, clearly agitated that this whole thing was already so much more difficult than a year earlier.

Richard threw the ball and David caught it. David had this way of making his face look like he was really thinking even when he wasn't, and as soon as he caught the ball, he did the face. I started laughing.

"Is something funny, Rod?" Carr had no choice but to ask.

"Sorry, I didn't know Rich had been drinking since the 90s."

Everyone laughed. This was a bad sign. The room was losing it.

"David," Carr turned his attention back to Dave, "new question. Pretend I'm handing you a drink tonight at a party. What do you do?"

Doc Carr then did a bit of improv, grabbing a fake glass and handing it to Dave. Dave took the imaginary drink and sat it on an imaginary table.

"No, thank you," David said.

It seemed like the right answer, but Doc didn't respond. Why no reply? That was the only answer made sense, and it was polite. In the world of 20 year olds attempting to prove they were grown, that was a very appealing answer to most older people. Not Doc Carr.

"David. David. That wasn't good enough. That was actually horrible."

We all looked confused.

"Hand me the drink," Doc requested.

David picked up the fake drink from where he fake placed it on the fake table and fake handed it to Doc Carr, who fake hurled it at the real wall.

"FUCK NO! I DON'T PLAY THAT SHIT!" Doc Yelled as the fake bits of fake glass shattered onto the floor.

The jarring nature of the response felt like he really threw something. I erupted in laughter, which sent half the room. This completely unnecessary action was only 45 seconds after Rich had announced he had been drinking since he was twelve. David said one 'no, thank you' and this negro threw a fake glass across the room. It was objectively hilarious.

"Is this funny to you, Rod?"

"Kindaaaa" I shrugged.

I was definitely a muckraker, but I also knew the rules. Keep it tight in times like these. I just absolutely couldn't. The more I thought about it the funnier it got.

"Get out," Carr said.

I looked at the head coach. He nodded. I looked at my teammates who were shaking their heads. They knew I just got a gift, even if it was a punishment.

I got my stuff together and I went home – to have a drink, in fact. Three hours later, around 1230 a.m., I started to get texts from the guys.

"Wow. You lucky motherfucker. They kept us here for four hours because of you," someone said.

It was unfair, to be sure. First the made up drinking premise, then the hypocrisy of it all, then the violent nature of the fake throw. Then to punish everyone by making them stay for hours? How the hell did the coaches expect anyone not to laugh?

Oh. This is why the seniors didn't let anyone talk. Noted.

I thought I had won the day, and maybe I did, but I did not win the war. The next morning I was expected to show up at 6am for a 2 on 1 session with Carr, the head coach, and myself. In fact, I came multiple days in a row. It was like a mini reconditioning camp.

I don't remember all of the meetings, but I'll never forget the second one. I was exhausted and upset that I had to keep coming in because Doc Carr threw a fake glass. On this day, they had a specific aim: they wanted to tell me that Ayinde Ubaka would start and Martin Smith would come off the bench to start the season.

"Cool," I said back, "gotcha."

I may have done finger guns.

"Do you agree with the decision?" they asked.

"Does it matter? You're the coach. I'm with whatever you say."

"Yeaaaa, but do you agree?"

"Yes. You're in charge."

"No, Do you think this is a good idea?"

They were unrelenting. They kept wanting me to say that I BELIEVED in what they were saying. Not only did I not, I couldn't have. I literally didn't even have the basketball IQ to make a decision like that. They just wanted to know that I believed. After a few rounds of this, I lost it.

"I just don't think any smart person got that way by blindly believing every dumb thing they were ever told."

I said this out of frustration and it was a mistake.

I think this was the point that they just stopped liking me as a person. I was good at basketball, very good, so they had to work with me, but I think they preferred guys who didn't think about what was happening. They were easier. There was nothing easy about me. I liked to know the 'why' and they didn't often give one.

For the next two weeks reconditioning continued. I'm unsure if it was out of spite or because they really wanted me to buy in, but either way I was there. If all the guys had to do was stay three hours long one day, they got off lucky. I had to pay off my laugh forever.

GAME DAY SCOUTING REPORT

VS

Different Dudes 27-1 (13-0)
Head Coach: Older Gentleman
Asst Coach: Slightly Less Old Gentleman

AI Generators 14-12 (3-11)
Head Coach: Hip Young Guy
Asst Coach: Slightly Older Hip Young Guy

12:00 PM NOON
"SPLASH ZONE" PAVILLION
SAN DIEGO, CALIFORNIA (THE WHITE PART)
TV:ESPN /ABC // WSDDRADIO872

this was assembled by an ops guy for some reason so thank him

KEYS TO VICTORY

RELENTLESS PRESSURE
BOX OUT
COMMUNICATION
STAR PLAYER RUNS THE PLAYS
GOOD PLAYER REMEMBERS THE PLAYS
SHOOTER MUST ALWAYS SHOOT
NOTHING GOOD HAPPENS AFTER MIDNIGHT
RUN THEM OFF THE THREE POINT LINE
NO FORNICATION THE NIGHT BEFORE
SOMEBODY ON THE BENCH CHEER VERY HARD
COACH GETS PAID ON TIME
REMEMBER THE TITANS
WHY ARE YOU ASKING ABOUT CLASS?
CONTEST AT THE RIM
ARRIVE NINE HOURS EARLY
PLAY DIFFERENT, DUDE!

#7 Star PLAYER   6"7" SF RH FR

Leads Team with 22ppg. 12 rpg
Last Game, against Michael Jordan, He scored Infinity
You Can't guard him
Can hit from anywhere, why bother?
Seriously, watch the film
McDonald's American and he has the shorts to prove it
Attended a school named after a liberal president
Self Given Nickname: "Him"

#44 He's GOOD   6"11" C? RH SR

Walking Double Double 11ppg 11.9 rpg
His biggest rebound was your mother
You're gonna get your ass kicked because you don't box out dummy
Hands measured at "nigga what?"
All American but from other publications and it counts
Loves video games and fishing, so you know he's crazy
Nickname: "Milfhunter"

#22 The SHOOTER   6"4" SG LH FR

Does one thing and one thing only 18ppg 0rb 0 ast
Can hit from slightly further than Star Player
Went to a HS named after something Catholic, then transferred to IMG
Walks around with a gun to prove how accurate a shooter he is
First Team All State, Hawaii
Favorite Player: No Chill Gill
Majors in Athletic Studies
Nickname: "Curl"

PRAY WE RUN THIS RIGHT WHEN TIRED

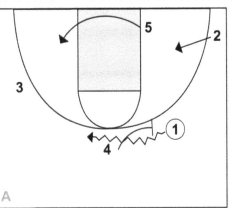

A

1 dribbles. Can't trust it.
Someone shoot.

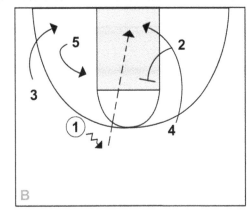

B

2 if necessary

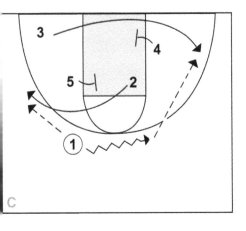

C

if necessary

San Diego

IF YOU'RE READING THIS, YOU
WERE ABLE TO AFFORD SEAT RIGHT
ON THE FLOOR!

THAT MEANS YOU, TOO, CAN MAKE
A DIFFERENCE, DUDE!

CONTACT THE SDD OFFICES TO LEARN
HOW TO DONATE YOUR MONEY.
WE CANT BE MEDIOCRE FOREVER!

GO DUDES!

HAMMERTIME

Korea had a huge learning curve socially. This was to be expected and no one was naive about the situation. With that, I actually think I did very well. I took Japanese classes in high school, which is distinctively not Korean, but the asian markets, the anime, the confucianism: it was similar enough for a head start. One thing I never fully got used to though, was the sauna. That shit was wild.

The Korean sauna 사우나 is basically just a room with a locker room, towels, an attendant, a scale, shaving shit, and, oddly, sodas and snacks for sale. There is usually another section behind a door where the water is, and that area is lined with showers, some weird sit down wash showers, and a couple large hot tubs. Add to that that everyone is fully nude and there are no walls and you get an interesting situation for sure. The first few times, despite what the coaches acclimated me to in college, shit was weird.

They just said the word "sauna" one day after a road game and then they took us. You should know that as a basketball player, I was just "taken" to shit I had no say in very often. This was no exception. I just hoped that I was correctly hearing "sauna" as we defined it. You know, like the infrared kind.

I clocked all this shit before I took my pants off. I know it's dumb, but some part of me was thinking we were too famous to be getting naked at a random sauna. I'm picturing the Sacramento Kings popping up in Citrus Heights at an LA Fitness and all going full Johnson for the paying customers. It was really like that.

My teammates just got naked and went in.

Naww fam.

I needed a minute, but they were fast. In and out. If I didn't just go, I'd just smell like ass the rest of the day. So, I decided to smell like ass and left.

But a few days later we were in the same situation. Once it was clear this was a cultural thing and not a one-off, I had no choice but to whip out the Toblerone and take a shower in front of so many Koreans. So, so many Koreans.

I'd like to say everyone just minded their business, but they absolutely did not. Most of these folks had never seen anyone not white or Korean in their lives. Now they're not only seeing a black guy, who's 208 centimeters tall (their measurement not mine), he's Nongu Sunsu (basketball player), and he's got a dick with more size and less hair then maybe any they've ever witnessed. I'm not even saying I'm big like that, but framing is everything. They were not well framed. I was.

"Wowww"

"Oaaaahhh"

"Ohoooohhh very big size!"

Koreans did not hold their tongue if they thought it was a good thing.

MY SHIT IS LARGER THAN AVERAGE DAMMIT. NICE.

I was getting a little cocky, (yea, I said it), but when I was out and getting dressed, my teammate looked directly at it.

"Oh! Wow! Big size!"

"Thanks?" I asked.

"You know Haenji? You big size. Haenji is Ha-ma!"

That was the day I learned that not only was a competitor in the league, Darren Haynes, bigger than me, but also that he carries what the Koreans refer to as a 'HAMMER.'

END OF DISCUSSION 2

The first day I got a basketball recruitment letter from UCLA, I knew life was going to be different. It wasn't because I could finally see myself playing college basketball. It wasn't because I knew I could attend any school in the country. It wasn't because all my hard work was finally paying off. It wasn't any of that.

It was when I walked the letter into AP English and sat it on my desk to do my usual stare and Jordan Phillips, a kid who sat next to me, leaned over and said, loudly:

"You're gonna get so much puss in college."

He repeated this every day for the rest of senior year. He was as vulgar as he was incorrect.

GET RICH OR DIE TRYIN

As a freshman in college, I was into some random shit. I had a Razor scooter that I took to and from campus (the to was cool, the from was horrible). I spent considerable time pining over this gray Sean Jean suit that sat in the window of a clothing shop on Bancroft. And I was consumed with adding ringtones to my Nokia 5190.

The 5190 was the most popular phone on the planet. It had Snake. It had texting. It had different color casings. It was lit. At some point during the previous year, you could now buy ringtones, too. The tones were basic as hell, but they were hot.

When I say basic, I mean they were MIDI tones. The phone beep didn't change in tone, it just beeped with specific timing to remind you of the song you were thinking of. I loved these. I love love loved these. I thought that ringtones were going to save the coddamn world.

Still, as much as I loved them, I couldn't afford them forever, so I found a way around paying for tones. There were these websites that gave instructions to manually enter the tones into the phone. It was a shitty process, but after I had successfully done it, I now had 50 Cent's chart topping hit, "Wanksta" as my ringtone. It went something like

Do-do-do-do-do-do-do do-do-do-do-do-do-do *buzzzz* *buzzzz*

Do-do-do-do-do-do-do do-do-do-do-do-do-do *buzzzz* *buzzzz*

I guess you had to be there.

One day we were in the locker room before practice and my phone rang. Wanksta came on and kinda got the room bopping a little bit.

"Ok Luda on that smart shit," someone may have said. Maybe not. They said this often so it's hard to index.

Joe Shipp, contender for Pac 10 Player of the Year, perked up a bit.

"Aye Luda… That's what's up," he said in a tone so low I could barely hear him.

He had the smoothest, softest voice, and I could never tell if it was real or if he knew ladies liked him sounding like low volume LL Cool J (LVLLCJ).

A few weeks later, we were getting dressed before playing Oregon at home. Joe walked by and everyone was gasping. He had the new Motorola with the color screen. Not the RAZR, this was before that, but it was still dope. No one had ever seen a color screen on a phone before.

I looked down at my Nokia. Its screen was just green and black. The case, although bright blue, now seemed colorless. Snake? That man now had Tetris. He was the king of the castle, and I was but its jester. Yet, I still had my tones. I let it play.

Do-do-do-do-do-do-do do-do-do-do-do-do-do *buzzzz* *buzzzz*

Do-do-do-do-do-do-do do-do-do-do-do-do-do *buzzzz* *buzzzz*

Guys bopped a little bit as Coach walked in to calm us down.

Still got it, Nokia.

Coach laid out the game plan and what not. It was the normal pregame hyperbole. Oregon had these players that we should be DEATHLY afraid of. Our guys, although good, were ALWAYS susceptible to defeat. And effort? Yea. We were going to need effort.

Break!

I literally don't remember the game at all. But when we came back at halftime, everything proceeded like it had before the game as Coach settled in to deliver the 'good news bad news' of the first half.

Right as he was about to speak, 50 Cent's Number One Hit Single, "In Da Club" started playing. Not some MIDI shit, but the song song. Everyone lost their damn minds. We were gigging and going dumb for like four seconds. Everybody was feeling it.

"Hey!" Coach yelled. Oh yea. Right. We were in a game. "Who's music is that?"

Joe looked up with a smirk.

"Oh shit," voice sexy as ever with a slight hint of laughter, "my bad. Let me get that."

Ho clapped his phone shut and looked up again, with a smirk.

WHEN WE SAW IT WAS HIS PHONE. HOLY SHIT. WE LOST IT. WE ABSOLUTELY LOST IT.

That was the day Joe Shipp finally became president.

WE DON'T DIE

I was drafted by the Austin Toros of the D-League out of college. I remember I was at JGant's house at the time in SF, watching results come in online. I'd been staying on the floor of his childhood bedroom for a solid month while I was waiting to find out what my basketball future would look like.

It was fun, but also I'm too big to be on my best friend's floor for a damn month. I was taken somewhere in the 6th round, and when it popped up on the screen, he and I drank some vodka and celebrated. It was time to go.

When I got to Austin, all of it was overwhelming. As a rookie, the game was faster than I was, and the learning curve was steep. The head coach, Dennis Johnson, was a very nice man, but one with a job to do. So while I did make the final roster, I hardly played after that. Looking back I'm sure he had a plan for me, but in hoops there was no time to waste so my agent got me up out of there.

DJ addressed me before I left. I hardly remember the conversation, but he was very supportive. He said something to the effect of it was a numbers game in Austin and he believed in me. Then, the Toros released me and I began my journey as a Dakota Wizard.

A month later I got a call from an old teammate in Austin.

"Aye man. Just wanted to let you know. DJ passed this morning."

My heart dropped to the floor. I had just seen him. He was so kind and full of life.

I guess they played a little one on one after practice and he collapsed during the game. When I asked how they were sure he was gone, he replied bluntly.

"He pissed himself and we all know that means it's over."

To that point, I had never considered what dying would actually look like. I learned then both how swift and how jarring a sudden death can be in the basketball world. Everyone felt it so differently than whatever I had experienced previously. We were the gold standard of health and athletic achievement. WE DON'T DIE. Except, we do.

Since then, several coaches and players have passed and not a single one felt like it was their time.

DEAD SERIOUS

In 7th grade, after years of baseball glory, it started to feel like I should be a basketball player with all this size. I was about 5'11" at the time (I could now see on top on the refrigerator) so I was one of the tallest kids in my class. The social pressure was real.

One day a bulletin went up at school announcing tryouts for the Oak Crest Waves basketball team. I went and signed up and did the tryout. I wore jeans because I didn't have any other clothes that worked for basketball. I should have felt embarrassed by that, but I don't remember it feeling that way. Other kids wore similar stuff except for the serious players who had been on travel teams for years. Since I wasn't on any team, jeans were what it was going to be. I made the team somehow and basketball was back in my life.

I was much taller than a lot of my competition, but I had no skill whatsoever. Some games would be dominant, and others would be horrible. Our rival school, Earl Warren Jr High, beat us by 50 points or something like that, in large part because they had five or six guys my height or taller who could actually play.

It was these games coupled with a local news report about a 6'10" 8th grader named Tyson Chandler up north, that I led me to think that I'd probably not be that good at basketball in the long run. How could I? I wasn't the tallest, fastest, or most skilled. I was a kid who thought Ginuwine was a lady until he saw the music video.

After that school year, my mother was not happy with how my education was unfolding and decided to move me to the school she was teaching at. She transferred me to Earl Warren, the school that beat us the year before by 50 points.

Being at this school gave me a renewed sense of ambition. The team was good and the coaching was better, so I thought I could turn it all around. Earl Warren has a Boys and Girls Club attached to it, so every day I'd go to the club and play basketball against the other kids.

At this point I was 6'1" and really starting to separate myself height-wise. Because of this, I was beginning to become someone who looked good against bad competition. My confidence started to skyrocket. I felt like I was ready to take on this new challenge and try out for the Earl Warren 8th grade team.

When I showed up to the tryout, it was clear that I had been only dominating the regular kids. The kids that were actually on the team were… Well, they weren't regular. There were three guys who stood 6'5" and the point guard, Kyle Cech, was 5'11" and had all the tools. Despite that, I still felt like I could make the team if I just went hard like I had been doing after school.

I laced up my two year old basketball shoes. They still felt capable enough after all this time, but they were too small. My mother said I would wear them until only rubber remained, and then she would turn that into erasers so I could use them in school again, to learn the value of basketball shoes. I did value them greatly as a result. I thought I may never get another pair.

I threw my Miller's Outpost jeans on, which had holes in them from my battles after school, and went out on the court. Everyone laughed at me. The new (black) kid came in jeans and shoes with holes in them. And he was dead serious.

Forget the laughs. Just play the game.

The coach who was running the tryout split up the teams for a scrimmage and we were off. I was in for the jump ball. The ball went up and I hit it first! It bounced around to some other kids and back to me. I grabbed it and took off, dribbling around defenders, crossing one over along the way until there was no one in my peripheral. I laid in the easy layup with a smile and looked at the coach to check his level of satisfaction. He had a big smile on his face too as he blew the whistle.

"Rod. Wrong way. Your basket's that way."

Everyone started dying with laughter. I scored on the wrong basket. My tryout was essentially over before it started. I, in fact, was not the first player to make the team in a pair of Miller's Outpost jeans. I did not make the team at all.

The fact that I didn't make the team wasn't the worst part. The worst was that I became known as "Wrong Way Rod" at my new school, a name people still call me to this day.

BONUS

Months later, Jared Dudley and I were shooting around at Skyline Elementary which sat across the street from Earl Warren. It had lower baskets to accommodate younger kids, so sometimes the middle schoolers would head over to practice dunks.

Jared was a 7th grader at Earl Warren at the time who didn't make the team either, for whatever reason. On this day it was just us two.

"I'm switching schools. These white people can't stand my game," Jared said after making a layup as the sun set over Solana Beach.

"Yea. One day they'll see," I said back.

A THREE HOUR TOUR

When we got to Beijing, I was seriously overwhelmed. Not only was this my first trip to Asia, I was traveling with the Pacers and we were there to play the 'Melo Nuggets. The plan was to play two games: the first in Taipei, which had already been played, then another in Beijing. Although these were preseason games, not everyone gets to play theirs in Asia, so I was feeling it.

Truth be told, my agent and I were hoping that exposure in Asia would be good for me. Either I would just make the Pacers, or Chinese and Korean teams would get a closer look at what I could do. Win-win, we thought. The issue was that I didn't play at all in Taipei, so I assumed I wasn't going to play again in Beijing. That's foolish, but our bodies protect us like that. It's brutal finally getting into the room and not getting any playing time to prove yourself. We learn to not get our bodies too worked up.

The day before we were supposed to play, a lot of the WAGs had put together a plan to hit the silk road for some low cost luxury knockoffs. I found this odd. They had so much money, why would they want knockoffs?

"No you don't understand," one of them explained to me,"this is where they make the shit. It's real, it's just not 'legal' to put the real brand on the bags."

It was satiating enough of an excuse. I didn't have real Louis money, but I had Fake Louis Per Diem that would do just fine. The only issue was that they were worried about the timing. We had to be back for a banquet with David Stern by 5pm. It was 2pm.

To me, there was plenty of time. Usually my concern would be fatigue from running around all day, but I wasn't even playing in the game, so that was moot. I jumped in the taxi with the WAGs and we headed the three miles to the Silk Road. When we arrived, it was 2:30.

We have so much time. They're trippin.

Once I was in, I worked fast. While the WAGs were taking their sweet time, I was browsing with speed and efficiency. I had my eyes on a couple things in particular: a Louis Vuitton laptop bag and a clutch/purse situation for Madison. Once I found the items, a green laptop bag and a white Marc Jacobs, I had to haggle just a bit to get those prices down to a number that felt like I was the winner. You get it.

I checked my phone. It was now 350pm. Perfect. I had over an hour to get back and change before the event. No problem at all. I walked outside and hailed a taxi. I took a seat and started doing dumb shit on my phone. A half hour later I finally looked up.

I've been in this bitch for a minute. We close?

We had moved all of forty feet. It was now 4:20 and we had moved forty feet.

THE FUCK IS THIS?

I did some quick math and realized there was no way I was going to make it back in time if I didn't exit the vehicle. I literally just jumped right out. I don't remember if I paid. It didn't matter. I just got out and started running in a direction I felt the hotel was located. I really couldn't tell where we were, but I knew it was within three miles.

There were no google maps, and if there were, it definitely wouldn't have been reliable there.

I was in a panic, looking for anything that would get me back. Finally, I saw a subway station. I checked the time and it was 4:31.

FUCK FUCK FUCK.

I ran down into the station, fake luxury shit bouncing everywhere, and of course all the signs were in Chinese. When I tell you I have no idea how I deciphered the machine or the map, I mean it. I think I may have just gotten lucky. There was no way to tell where shit was except Tiananmen square, because that took up so much space on the map. That helped orient me a bit, but really though, I had no clue. This was throwing darts into the wind.

With my ticket to somewhere in hand, I went down to the train arrival area and waited. It was 4:37pm. Not only did I need to get back to the hotel, I had to change into a full suit, then go to a banquet area across the complex and meet the team before they took the stage at the Stern presentation. I hadn't really considered all the circumstances before then, because it was moot. Now, with potentially my NBA career in the balance, I was at the whim of this train and whatever its stops may be.

As I waited, which wasn't long, thousands of Chinese people flooded the station around me. There were so many folks trickling in that I couldn't move side to side. This happened too fast.

If we have to go in two groups, I'm pushing for the first one. No time for games.

When the train came at 4:40, the doors opened and the train was COMPLETELY full. I have literally never seen a train so full. My heart dropped. How many trains would I have to wait for before one had space? I really didn't know the Beijing demographics.

I really don't know the Beijing demographics.

As soon as the train's doors opened, the flood around me rushed in. Not a single person got off. I really can't even explain the physics. Not even a little bit. I was like rushed onto a train from the sheer force of the group moving that once. And that train was so full I didn't see how even one person could get on, let alone hundreds.

Shit, maybe another thousand people boarded this train. It was so tight that I couldn't move any limbs. I couldn't feel my body. Nothing at all. For real, if my dick had gotten hard for any reason, so many people would have been violated. It was that tight. I couldn't reach my phone to check the time. I didn't even know if I still had a phone. Someone could be groping me, robbing me, and planting evidence all over my body and I would have no idea.

I counted the stops because I couldn't tell what direction we were going. Three stops seemed appropriate. Getting off the train was even more difficult. The Chinese folks didn't just move. They didn't even hardly look at me. They just stood there, kinda sad looking, just waiting to be pushed out of the way like zombies who quiet quit. It was super weird.

When I made it off the train and out of the station, I looked up. There was the mother fucking Ritz Carlton, thank 6 lb 8 oz baby Jesus. I didn't look at my phone, I just ran inside. I didn't see anyone in the lobby, which was a bad sign. Wherever people were, they were clearly already there.

I changed into my suit and checked my phone. 4:57. I hadn't showered for shit, but there was no time to consider that. I ran back down and literally sprinted to the banquet hall. As soon as I walked in, David Stern was standing at a podium.

"And now, it's my pleasure to introduce the Indiana Pacers!"

Everyone started clapping. I scanned the room and saw my suited teammates stage right, starting to make their way to the stage. I walked calmly, but in a full sweat, to the end of the group right before the guy in front of me took the stage.

I walked up there and sweated this suit out in front of a few hundred Chinese diplomats. But holy shit, I was there. David didn't need to fire me. I exhaled. I made it.

And I got the goods. Bless up.

The Louis bag broke about eight months later. I was walking in the airport and the strap just snapped and my laptop fell to the ground, denting the edge. The "Marc Jacobs" bag I got Madison broke before December. She called me to say she took it to the Marc Jacobs store for repairs. I'm unsure what they told her, but we never talked about the bag again.

YOU'RE JUST YOUNG

Right out of college, when I was training in Sacramento, we were all so broke that we did everything together. The couple guys with money would often host a bunch of us for food or some beers or whatever. Shouts to Matt Barnes for being one of those dudes who invited hella random broke guys with nothing to lose to his house repeatedly. That's bold.

Anyways, we weren't at Matt's this day. I don't know whose house we were at, but I know that at some point someone put 'TWO GIRLS ONE CUP' on a laptop and everyone was watching and laughing.

I refused to look. The guys quickly picked up on this because they were emotional snipers.

"You don't wanna see?"

"Nah man, that's hella gross." I said, still in my Bay phase.

They all laughed.

"You're just young," one of them said. "Watch, by the time you're my age you gonna be into all this shit. Trust me."

He was 27, so I can firmly say now that I'm 38 that no, I did not ever get into 'TWO GIRLS ONE CUP.'

20 years later and I still don't get why we, a room full of dudes, wanted to watch it together at the same time. Shoulda been called "Seven dudes, watching two girls, do weird shit in one cup."

HAIR DAWG

My first season in Korea was unique because I was out there trying to figure out a lot. My old D-League coach, Jay Humpries, hadn't given me much advice before I went out there. The best thing he told me was to get the Korean fans on my side, so I was trying to workshop dunk celebrations in real time until something stuck. The military style salute it was.

My American teammate, Victor Thomas, also tried to provide as much context as possible. It was mostly little things, like which restaurants to avoid, or how to deal with the coaching staff. But there was one lesson that stood out above the rest because I witnessed it play out in real time.

We were heading out to Itaewon, a place I would refer to as America Town. The area is near one of the oldest American military installations in Asia. There are generations of Americans who have grown up there, as well as Koreans who chose to live nearby because they were into Western food and culture. There were also so many soldiers there it was unreal.

The soldiers aren't the point of the story, but on this first night out in Itaewon I learned a lot about who is fighting for our country. They're

18, have no idea what they're doing, and they are super disruptive to the local society – fighting and occasionally assaulting the locals.

Because of this (and racism) there are many bars Americans aren't allowed in. This has changed a lot, but back then, we had to announce we were not in the military and show our ID or many places wouldn't let us in. Often we could just point to our beards as a sign we were civilians. The white school teachers did not have this problem.

Because of *that*, according to Victor, the best spots in town were all the spots where military was allowed. They played hip hop music, often new shit I hadn't even heard, and the party would feel more like a hood experience in the US than a dirty bar in Korea. It was safer, though, because no one had any guns except the MP's. I think.

I forget the name of the bar Victor took me to, but it was a very popular one. When we got to the bottom of the flight of stairs that lead into the entrance, there were green laser lights everywhere, bouncing off the faces and bodies of hundreds of black people. I may as well have been in South Carolina instead of South Korea.

We pulled up to the bar and this woman was already seated in one of the seats next to us. She was holding a bottle I was unfamiliar with. Victor saw me looking at the bottle.

"That right there," he started, "is the devil's juice. Soju. Have you heard of it? I've been here enough to know that it destroys white women."

He got slightly closer to my face to make his point.

"Destroys! That woman there next to us is going to leave fucked up. Trust me."

He gestured to the woman, holding what I now knew was a bottle of Soju. It was a stern warning. So stern, in fact, that it was a year before I even tried it. I wasn't sure what it was, but I knew that Victor said it was devil juice. That was enough for me.

We partied and whatever, taking shots of this and that as the trap music and the green lasers were going off. People were drinking all sorts of creative shit out of buckets and everything. Korean bars definitely leaned into the spring break feel of 2000's Cancun.

While we were making our way out to go home, we walked up the stairs to exit the spot, and that same woman was there eyeballing me hard. Despite Victors' best predictions, she was fine! Sober and very much into me. I wasn't so much into her, though. She was kind of cute, but I was more fascinated that she had consumed an amount of soju that Victor had assured me would kill her, and here she was offering us another shot before we left.

"I don't see why not," I said to both of them.

This was dumb as hell.

"Great!" she said as we turned back down the stairs.

Victor waited. As soon as I got down two steps out of twelve, she must have drunkenly lost her balance behind me or something because she fell. It was a complete free fall and she headed right for me. I tried to avoid her as she was falling, but she grabbed my shirt. Instinctively, I reached out for hand rails to stop myself, to stop both of us from falling. I'll never forget the horror I felt as I realized there were none. We were going down. Hard.

We literally skipped all the remaining stairs and slammed directly on the ground right in front of the bar. She landed on her back, I landed on top of her, knee to the ground first. I was stunned and it took me a minute to collect myself. I rubbed my throbbing knee. It was going to be a problem.

Before I could fully gather myself, maybe a half second after we hit, some dude was standing there over us and gave me an important update:

"Ayo this bitch had a wig on!"

I looked over and the woman, who was also still dazed and looking as drunk as Victor had predicted, was missing her hair. Where the hell was it?

Oh.

"Aye I got this bitch hair, dawg!"

The military kids were playing with her wig like it was capture the flag. She just laid there, confused and drunk, unaware of the situation.

You know what? I'm good.

I got up and my knee was in tremendous pain, but there was no time to consider that. I climbed up the stairs with no rails to help me, leaving her down there to fend for herself. I didn't need to see the end of that episode.

"What I tell you Rod? That. Is. Devil's. Juice."

Victor stood there and watched it all unfold just to make sure I learned the lesson.

Touche.

CUT 3

I flew into Puerto Rico on a red eye from Los Angeles and immediately drove three hours into the jungle to play a game that night against a 300-something lb. monster Robert "Tractor" Traylor.

I played horrible. I was on a flight home the next day.

I did get to see a child ride a horse into a bar as the DJ spun Daddy Yankee, though.

EMAILS FROM BILL 4

From: BILL

Fwd To: Rod Benson

Sent: 7/14/2010 8:46:43 A.M. Eastern Daylight Time

Subj: Re: Rod

???@turner.com>

To:

Bill

Tue, Jul 13, 2010 at 12:00 PM

Hi Rod,

My name is —--- and I am contacting you on behalf of producer —-----,

with The Cartoon Network. We have a new NBA show called —-----

airing this fall and we would like you to be apart of it. Would you please

email me a phone number we can reach you at so we can talk more about the

show. I look forward to speaking with you!

???@turner.com

(404)--------

THE EVITE

After a big breakup during the Las Vegas summer league in 2009, I decided to head down to LA instead of back up to Sacramento where my ex would be. I figured I'd stay a few days and then make my way back up when the time was right.

On that first night in LA, Tommy, an old college basketball friend, invited me to a house party. Tommy is about my size, had been playing professional basketball overseas, and had long lamented my decision to play in the D-League because he didn't like seeing me broke. He'd been played in various countries and earned enough money to buy himself a fancy SUV and rent an apartment out in Malibu. I can't lie, I was very jealous of him at this time because he was really living.

I arrived at a cool loft downtown and Tommy immediately introduced me to Matt, whose apartment it was, and Eric, who was Tommy's best friend. Matt was a cool cat who lived in one of the dopest lofts I had seen to that point. He was chill and eventually got back to the other folks in the room. Eric, on other hand, walked right up to me and said he was familiar with the BOOMTHO Movement and that he was excited to meet me.

He stood 6'5" and told me he used to play pro hockey. He then pulled open a laptop and showed me a video of him losing a hockey fight. As he was getting knocked out, he laughed and dared me to take a shot of vodka. I figured whoever this kid was, he was cool with me! I left that night with a new friend.

As that summer went on, I was supposed to go back to Sacramento but I didn't. I stayed in LA with Tommy and Eric who I would see pretty much every day. Tommy was located in Malibu so I stayed with him on his couch or floor and every night we would drive into Hollywood and go to different hotels like the Mondrian or the W, party for a night, and then go back to Malibu.

This was pretty much every day in August of 2009. When we weren't turning up, we were working out at Pepperdine with their men's basketball team to stay in shape for the upcoming season.

Eventually, Tommy started ditching us at the end of the night with no explanation, leaving us to take long taxis home or stuck at a hotel because we didn't have a key to his house. It was frustrating at first, but eventually it got a little suspicious because we started asking who he kept ditching us for and he would lie and say it was no one.

After a few weeks of this, he finally revealed to us that he'd been seeing a woman in Redondo named Michelle. He insisted that she was cool and that we should come down to Redondo with him to meet her. So Tommy, Eric, and I jumped in the SUV with him and headed down to meet her on a Saturday afternoon.

Michelle is what I can only describe as a crazy person. I hate saying the word crazy but man alive, she's a crazy person. First of all, her entire apartment was pink. The shelves were pink. The walls were pink. The bedding was pink. Everything. But it was not tastefully done. It was not an Instagram experience. It was just pink in a way that felt like a four year old might do it. It was hard to move because there was pink shit and very low to the ground furniture everywhere with weed burns in it. The black burns did compliment the wallpaper, I suppose.

Michelle herself was as high as a person can be. In fact she was so high that I couldn't tell if she was really not a bright person or if she was just a weed zombie. Looking back it was probably a combination of both but at the time it just registered to me as everything about this is annoying.

I'm out in Redondo, a place I don't go often, sitting here in a pink room with someone who has been ruining my friendship, having one of the least intelligent conversations of my life. I'm cordial enough, but when it's time to go I make it clear to Tommy and Eric that I don't need to see more. That was my last time visiting the pink apartment.

As basketball season approached, it was the year of the Great Recession so overseas team budgets had crumbled. This complicated what my choices could be for that 2009-10 season. I hadn't done well in France, so I didn't have a ton of juice, and even if I did, who could pay me what I had established I was worth? Very few teams at all. So although I hadn't been keen on the D-League for that upcoming season, it felt like the only move I could really make.

Tommy was feeling similar pressure, so we both decided to sign back in the D-League with hopes of landing on an LA based team. Unfortunately, my rights were not my own, so as much as I wanted to play for the LA Defenders, I pretty much had to go back to the Reno Bighorns.

I wasn't upset though, because I had a good relationship with the Bighorns and we were a competitive team. Tommy was blessed to make it on in LA so he stayed in town with Eric. It was at this time that Eric and I had begun having secret talks about how much we didn't like Michelle. We agreed that next summer would be best without her.

Feeling confident after our chat, I made it clear to both Eric and Tommy that I didn't like Michelle and that if we could not see her next summer when we were all in the offseason again that would be great. Obviously Tommy didn't like me saying this but it needed to be said. There was no resolution.

As the season got going, it became clear that Michelle was not going anywhere. In fact, Michelle and Tommy were now closer than ever. I wasn't nearby so I didn't see it myself, but Eric would call or text me with updates all the time and the updates always felt bleak. He'd call and say something like "I'm trying to get Tommy to do other stuff, but all he does is go to basketball and then go straight to Michelle's. I swear I'm trying, though."

Eventually our only choice became to hope that something went wrong in their relationship. Looking back, it was out of pocket to wish someone's very happy love life to crash and burn. We were mostly just unhappy that our boy was now gone from the streets, but it still did feel like we were doing the right thing for everyone involved.

One day in February, Eric called me.

"We have a problem," he started. "You're on break for D-League All Star weekend, right? Well so is Tommy and he drove to Las Vegas with Michelle and I tagged along. And, well, Tommy and Michelle had just decided to get married."

"Ayo! What?!" I was having an immediate meltdown.

"I tried my best," Eric pleaded, "but that they were playing slots when Michelle suggested that if they hit the jackpot, it would be a sign to get married. I guess she was joking, but then they hit something like $500 on a nickel slot. I was shook, man. I told them that it was crazy but they shouldn't really get married. They agreed, but then she said double or nothing would be the real sign. So they played again and on the next pull, they hit $1500. They looked into each other's eyes believing they had received a sign from God that this was meant to be."

What in all hell is happening? That's a lot of information to receive in short order.

"This is a lot of information to receive in very short order," I started. "They're actually going to go through with it?"

"It's already done. I was just calling to let you know."

I wanted so badly to be upset, but how could I be? If that story really went down the way he described, who was I to stand in the way of true love? I had to get out of the way. It was then that I decided to let it go and focus on my own happiness.

That next offseason Tommy was essentially nonexistent. He and his wife were always busy and never available. Conversely, I had gotten back with my ex, so that summer it was me, her, and Eric kicking it every day, hoping that Tommy would show up. After a couple months of this, my hatred of their relationship came back. If them being together also meant that I would never see him again, then this was definitely not going to be good.

We got him out exactly one day that summer. Tommy came over to my ex's place and we were catching up with Eric and it felt like old times. It was truly great, but at some point in the night, he got a call and went outside to take it. A few minutes later, we heard the SUV engine fire up, and he drove off without saying goodbye.

That next season brought a lot of changes. I had a good D-League showing and summer league and I signed in Korea for the first time. Tommy had the same experience that season and he signed in Japan. It was completely coincidental that we both signed in Asia at the same time. Although we didn't talk as often as before, and we definitely didn't see each other in person, we did stay connected. I was happy that Tommy and Michelle were going to move to Japan and start a new life. I still didn't like her and I still didn't want them together but what could I do at this point? It had been a full year and I wasn't in the position to get in the way of their lives.

Another coincidence was that a former teammate of mine, Isaiah, ended up signing on the same team as Tommy in Japan. Isaiah and I were close so he called me when he signed and said how excited he was to play with Tommy. He mentioned that he used to see the pictures of Tommy and me partying and he thought Tommy would have a dope playing buddy out in Japan. Isaiah liked that because he had never been to Asia and was looking for friendly faces. I told him Tommy was that dude and that for sure they would end up getting close. Isaiah was excited about the season and its possibilities as we got off the phone.

It was at this time that Tommy stopped really returning texts and calls and became a ghost. I'm not going to say that we never spoke, but maybe that season we spoke exactly one time. I blamed it all on her. I was speaking with Eric almost every day from the US and I couldn't get my good friend on a line from Japan.

Towards the end of the season I got a Skype call from Isaiah. I asked Isaiah how it's been going with Tommy assuming they were pretty close by that point. Isaiah sighed and said Tommy was not who he thought he was.

"Honestly, bro," he started, "I thought we were gonna have fun and be in these streets and whatnot but not at all. In fact, I don't fuck with him at all. No one does. I really thought cause you're boys he'd be cool, but absolutely not. And really it's all a joke at this point."

I asked him to explain, so he did.

"Bro all they do is fight all the time. Tommy and Michelle are crazy people. They yell and make everyone uncomfortable. I just stay out of their way you know, but that's not the worst part. Bro you know all the players' wives talk and gossip and my girl said that Michelle hates Tommy. She said Michelle is just trying to make it to Valentines Day or something because then the marriage can't be annulled. I guess she can file for divorce and get more money if they make it past that date. I don't know all the details but it's something like that."

I looked at the calendar and it was February 18th. I must have screamed at Isaiah.

"Why didn't you tell him this?!"

"Bro," he said while shaking his head, "like I said, I don't fuck with him! We don't talk! Why would he even listen to me? But that's not even the worst part anyway."

Oh Jesus Christ what else?

"Michelle fucks dudes on the other teams when they come to town and everyone in the league knows it. Tommy is basically the butt of everyone's jokes. I feel bad for him but he does his own dirt too, plus I don't fuck with him so it is what it is. I'm really telling you because maybe you can tell him or figure this out or whatever cause it's all bad out here."

As soon as I got off the Skype call, I called Eric and told him every-thing. Eric was absolutely shook. I was too, but I felt optimistic because we finally had the ammo to help get this man out of this relationship a year and a half after we first tried. Season was nearly over so we both decided that the best time to relay this information to him might be when we were all back in LA just in case he needed friends in the room.

So we did exactly that. We let the time pass until we were all back in town for the offseason and then we tried to set up a night out with Tommy. This was difficult just like it was the summer before because Tommy was still inaccessible. It took us maybe a month or two to finally get him out. When we did, the plan was that we would go out to a club and then convince him to come back to our crib after. Then Eric would break down for him what we had learned because Eric and Tommy were still and always had been better friends than I was with either of them.

As planned, we went out to the club and came back to my apartment in Downtown LA late. We were sitting in the bedroom joking and laughing for a while until there was a break in the laughter. Right then I looked up at Eric.

It's time.

He looked back at me and did a slow nod, then he turned to Tommy and said "Rod has something to tell you."

I looked at Eric with a scowl.

How the hell is he gonna flip this script when we practiced this whole situa-tion for months?

Tommy was now looking at me waiting for me to speak so I just laid it all out for him. I told him every single thing that Isaiah had broken down for me and I could see his face just melt into sadness, then disap-pointment, and then anger.

He excused himself from the room and he left. We were thinking he had gone home until we could hear his voice through the window coming from outside. We realized he was on the rooftop screaming at the phone saying things like "you're fucking dead to me Michelle! Your fucking dead to me! In Japan, Michelle? In Japan? Are you kidding me Michelle? You're f****** dead to me!"

Tears were streaming down his face when we got to the roof to check on him. He didn't stay much longer once he realized we could hear him, though. When he left it felt brutal, but Eric and I looked at each other with relief because although it took a year and a half, we finally did it. Maybe now Tommy could find real happiness and get his basketball back on track after a bad season.

Something that was always odd about the situation was that Tommy and Michelle had actually been married for over a year. So there was no turning back from that. But they did want to have a big ceremony with friends and family that was local. In what I can only describe as a very weird choice, they sent out their wedding invitations via Evite. I was getting email reminders to RSVP but I hadn't done so because I knew that Eric and I were about to drop the bomb that would end it all. We knew we had achieved our goal when we got "event canceled" email updates the next day. It was kind of funny, but also a reminder that life would soon reset back to normal and we could get back to hooping and turning up.

About 3 days later I got another email from Evite saying the event was back on. I walked over to Eric's room and we had a conversation about how it seemed there was nothing we could do. We did our best and gave him all the information we could. There was truly no other play to make here.

Over the next week or two, I would get an email saying the event was back off, then I would get one that said it was back on, and so on. It was hilarious every time, but it did feel like this ceremony really might not happen. Eric and I were making no plans to attend even though Eric was supposed to be the best man. There was just too much confusion at that point.

One day not too long after the last "it's canceled" Evite, I had a meeting in Portland, so I got on a flight and headed up. While I was in said meeting, which was around 9pm at night, Eric called me nearly a dozen times. I let the calls go to voicemail because I was busy, and because Eric would often call about small things like running into Tom Green at a bar. It didn't feel important. I did try to call him back, but there was no answer.

The next day I got back to LA and when I walked into the house Eric was sitting at the dining table looking a bit worrisome. I asked him what was wrong because it clearly had something to do with Tommy. My thought was that the wedding was now back on and the idea of being the best man was becoming a burden. Eric said that this was a different issue so I dropped my bags and took a seat.

"So," he started, "Tommy and Michelle I guess got into a big fight recently and it got bad."

"Ok? That happens all the time. So what?" I asked in response.

"Well Michelle's sister was there as this one was happening and I guess Tommy got very insulting. He was calling Michelle a whore and other crazy shit because of everything that she did in Japan. And the reality is Tommy was also doing dirt in Japan and I guess Michelle knew about it the whole time. So that was part of the anger that day because the sister thought that Tommy was being unfair and rude and also obviously protecting her sister.

I guess at some point Tommy said something like 'at least I didn't f*** half of Japan' to which Michelle's sister responded 'oh yeah? Well Michelle fucked Eric."

I just stopped the entire story right there and yelled "what did you just say?!"

"Yea. I fucked Michelle. Back in '09 in Redondo right after you left to go to Reno."

I sat there for a good 30 seconds shaking before questions followed.

"How in the hell could you not tell me this Eric? How in the world did you keep this a secret? We've been trying for a year-and-a-half to break these two up and you knew this the whole time and didn't say it once?!"

He sat there just looking ashamed.

"We thought we were going to take it to the grave, man."

"This is the dumbest shit I've ever heard in my life. There was so much that we could have done or said. We have been pushing this whole story from Japan and you couldn't even say this? But alright. It happened. That's what you called to tell me that right?"

"Yeah man. It was crazy when he called me and I needed help. I don't know what to do. The wedding is off again and now Tommy hates me."

"Well I would love to feel sorry for you but I don't. What will happen is what's going to happen man I don't I don't know what to say."

Two mornings later Eric knocked on my door and asked if I wanted to work out. He used to knock on my door and ask me if I wanted to work out most mornings. I would always say no because I wasn't trying to do random workouts, especially not while hungover as often as we were back then. But on this day I actually had a good amount of energy so I told him to give me a minute and I'd join him.

He looked a little confused because he was used to me saying no. A quarter second later he said "okay I'm just going to run an errand real quick and when I get back we can go."

"Nonsense," I replied sharply. "I'll be ready in 5 seconds. I'm just going to throw some shorts on real quick and then I'll drive us."

He was being weird.

"No no. It's fine I'll be right back!" he said as he literally ran out of the house.

I threw on shorts and a t-shirt which took me all of 15 seconds and I walked out expecting to see him, but he had already gone down the elevator. I went down to my car and I drove around the building to meet him. As I was driving around from the back of the building to the front I could see Eric in a full sprint running towards the front of our building. It looked crazy, so I just drove behind him slowly, watching him run down the street and eventually into the lobby of our building.

He handed an envelope to the front desk lady, breathed a sigh of relief, and then looked up and caught me outside looking at him through the car.

He nodded like he was expecting to see me there, came outside, gots in the passenger seat and said "are you ready?"

"I am absolutely not ready. What was that?"

"Oh I just had to leave something there for somebody," he said, shaking.

"That's not a good enough answer. What is going on here?"

Eric tried to breathe.

"Okay well, Tommy is still really mad and he said I owe him for all the times that he paid for me when we've been out. It's like a lot of different things but he wanted that money today by 10 am."

"How much money is it?"

"He said $5,000."

"WHAT?" I was screaming. "There's no way you're going to pay him $5,000 right now. There's no way."

"It's too late. I just left the money up there at the front desk. He and his cousin are coming right now and he said if he didn't get the money he's going to maybe kill me. I don't know if they're going to break my legs or something." Eric was clearly rattled and rambling.

"Look. Tommy has never once been that guy. Even as a basketball player he's not that guy." I looked at the clock. It was 9:58 a.m. "Just wait right here."

I walked into the building and up to our receptionist. I asked her if Eric had just handed her something. She pulled out an envelope and before she could fully explain, I said I needed it and I took it from her. I looked inside and sure enough there was $5,000 neatly tucked within. I walked back outside, popped my trunk, and I put it inside of my bowling ball bag. Then I got back into the driver seat and looked at Eric and he was freaking out and sweating. I could tell there was legitimate fear in his soul. He was actually really scared about what Tommy might do.

"What now?" Eric could barely get the words out. "He's coming here right now. Like what am I going to do, like what am I going to do?"

"Don't worry about it," I said as I put the car into Drive and pulled off.

As I was driving East on Wilshire, Tommy drove past us going West and somehow didn't see us. We could see him pull in front of the building exactly where I was just parked, but I kept driving.

Eric's phone rang. I could see that it was Tommy calling. Eric was freaking out and repeating the question "what do I do?" over and over.

I answered him calmly.

"There's so many reasons why you might not be able to get $5,000 cash, Eric. Say the bank placed a limit on you or maybe there's a weird hold or something. I don't know! Just make up some excuse that buys time because Tommy's not this guy. He just needs time because he is hurting."

Eric calmed down and answered the phone. I could hear Tommy's voice through the receiver just barely enough to hear him yelling. Eric looked at me and I looked back at him and gave a nod

We talked about this. Say anything about the bank.

Eric then looked down, looked up, and said "it was all Rod, man. He took the money and he wouldn't let me leave it for you. I tried my best to leave it for you. You know you've always been my homie and I would never do this to you, but it's Rod. He's the one out here trying to make this difficult like I'm so sorry."

I snatched the phone from his hand and hung it up and looked at Eric

You piece of garbage.

I drove to the car wash on Sunset near Echo Park and I ordered the fanciest car wash they have. They told me the wash was going to take three hours. I turned off Eric's phone and put it in the trunk as well, and we sat down for the three hours it took to wash my car.

What's wild is that Tommy didn't ask again. I don't think he ever followed up after that day. An hour after the car wash was done, we got one more notification from Evite. The event was canceled and never again was it back on.

I soon went back to Korea where I kept playing for another eight years. Tommy was more of a journeyman, but always found somewhere to get a paycheck, and Eric eventually moved out of town, ending our own tumultuous relationship. The three of us never kicked it together again.

JORDAN XI

"Are you hurt or are you injured?"

I don't remember the first time I was asked that question, but I then heard it thousands of times throughout the rest of my career. It was an important question to ask children, because they truly didn't know the difference. As adults, most never put themselves in a position to even consider the question. However, to people aiming to hurt one another professionally, the difference between being hurt and injured needed to be strongly labeled so that you could push your body to its true limit.

This was the toughest thing to understand from all sides. Trainers often would say that you could or couldn't push through something and it almost always felt like the opposite. Coaches would constantly look at you, ask you questions, and pressure you to get up or to come back as soon as possible. Fans always think the timeline is too long. I don't care if you take an elbow and are down 6 minutes or have to miss 6 games, fans are gonna be like "I took more elbows in the Korean War. Get up."

Eventually, as a player you aren't asking yourself if you're hurt or injured, but instead if you're a bitch or not. In my younger days, I tilted towards "bitch" more often. That means that I would really be hurt. Seriously hurt. And I would take myself out. Minutes later I was totally fine and ready to come back in. Nobody respected that shit. Bitch.

There was a drill in college called 'War.' War was a rebounding drill where the coaches put The Bubble over the top of the rim, a device designed to spur super random rebounds because it was covered in soft plastic spikes. I can not tell you how dumb this device was. It did not make me better as a rebounder, in large part because the bounces were unpredictable. In a real game, every rebound has a high amount of predictability, a fact I learned from Bill Russell.

Anyways, because the ball could go anywhere, the war drill wasn't about technique. It was about hitting people. I was skinny. Other guys were big. I must've taken (and given) hundreds of elbows to the teeth. We all have chipped teeth for the sake of that bitch ass drill. And every time I took a bow and needed a minute, I felt like a bitch.

In college, it was more that we didn't know our bodies, for better or worse. If I had a sore foot, I didn't know if my career was over or if I could play tomorrow. I had to fully rely on what the staff told me. All I can say is this led me to some choices I 100% would not make again. One of them being the shot I took at halftime of the Pac-10 tournament my Junior season. I still don't really know what I hurt, but I know I got a shot, came back, and still didn't play. If I wasn't going to play more than two second half minutes, I certainly didn't need an injection in the back of Staples Center.

The next day I woke up forgetting all about the shot. When I got up to go to the bathroom, I fell over. I couldn't walk. I wondered if that was that how I was supposed to feel the whole time. I tore my meniscus a few months later. Now I wonder if I actually tore it then or if it had been lingering since the shot?

But then I saw guys like Brian Wethers who was 22 and could hardly walk after every practice; taking every shot he could and living in a tomb of ice just for the chance to play.

Your ligaments don't matter, bitch. Get back in.

I think there is something about seeing guys worse off than us that leads us to make choices we absolutely shouldn't. I remember when I was in Austin, I saw Jay Will do a lot of things I wouldn't personally agree with. Nothing more on point than thinking he could beat the descending robotic arm of a paid parking lot in an Escalade ESV, the longest vehicle a man can buy and the second of two Escalade ESV's on the same ticket. I need to make this more clear. There were two cars. The first one, an escalade driven by James White, paid. Jay believed that he should try to make it on the same ticket without paying, so he hit the gas and the arm slammed down on the front of the 37 foot long car, scraping the car from the hood to the trunk on our way out. Man's was stubborn.

And still, when he was out there in his last games, being equally as stubborn trying so damn hard to come back, notching stat lines of 9 pts 11 ast 14 to, it didn't' feel as stubborn. It felt like you needed a bit of that to really be great. It made me feel like a bitch when I had a sore ankle. Maybe both were true.

I played with a 'legend' in Korea, Kim Joo Sung. He was probably the best player in the league for most of my time there, and this dude missed 45% of the games we played. With him in the game, we won 9 games out of 10 and with him out, 4 out of 7. So every single person, including me, badgered him every day.

The dude looked fine. He played great when he played. He would walk around and joke and smile. I assumed he had to be taking little mental breaks or something. Then one day I went with him because we both had MRI's on the same day. I saw his scans. The fact that the sawdust where his bones used to be had held up the way it had was amazing. I never questioned him again.

After internalizing these things over and over, it became clear that only I truly ever knew what was going on with my body and even then it wasn't 100% accurate. Blake Griffin saw me warming up slowly in 2010 and said "so your knees are done, huh?"

I looked at my knees, both in braces, and then back up at him.

"I hope not."

200

I went on to never need knee braces again and played eight more very athletic years. I just needed to lift more. Today, years out of basketball, I can likely jump higher than him. It was just a weird couple months.

In 2017 I fell on a rebound attempt and landed directly on my elbow. It got so swollen that I couldn't move my left arm at all for a few days. What was worse was that there was a cut on the elbow as well, leading it to leak pus out while I slept. LOTS OF PUS. Sharon dubbed it the "leaky elbow" and it became a genuine fear of hers that I would leak elbow juice onto her in the night.

Because of that I would sleep weird, making it worse. I would go into practice with an arm that wasn't healing as quickly as everyone else would like, meanwhile I was the one dealing with random elbow leakiness that seemed incurable. It didn't matter. I was being a bitch.

That same season I had a foot injury so bad that I took multiple of the shots I regretted from college, took trains up and down the Korean Peninsula visiting the best doctors, getting MRI's, scans, and tests of all kinds. There was no solid diagnosis. No one could figure it out. If anything, it got worse. They were about to release me.

"Did you change your shoes?" Kim Joo Sung asked the most basic question, via a translator. No one else had asked it, though.

I switched to Kobe's and my feet miraculously healed. He knew shit the doctors didn't, including that the new Jordan 11's were fucking me up. I was fine with the switch to Kobe's within two days.

All I can say after years of being hurt, everybody's right and everybody's wrong. The only question you can ask yourself is if you wanna be a bitch or not.

WIZZONATOR

When I was in college, we were drug tested sporadically. I didn't do any drug that could end up on a test, so I never paid much mind to it. I think we just urinated into a cup in the bathroom like anyone who goes to the doctor would do. I guess this meant it was also an easy test to beat? I don't know, but the fact that no one ever got caught amazes me.

I distinctly remember many of my professional drug tests, though, because them shits were not the same. The first one I had was with the Austin Toros. We had to get tested before the first practice of camp. I was dropped off at some medical facility that reminded me of an office park from the 80's.

When I walked into the health clinic doors, there were dudes everywhere. I had never met any of these people before, so every step of the way I was trying to understand who was on the team, who worked for the program, who was a doctor, etc. They all looked big. And mean. There was this seven foot white dude. I recognized him.

That's Brad Buckman. I recognize him.

Other guys I didn't know at all, but it felt like we were all posturing. Standing our very tallest. Trying to look like we didn't care, but of course we did. Some of us would be cut in a few days.

Everyone thinks I'm some big extrovert, and maybe I've grown into it, but back then I'd never say a word in rooms like this. I'd sit around, stone faced, posturing myself, showing as little emotion as possible. If I did show emotion, it was in response to a text message.

I've got important shit going on.

When they called my turn to do my test, I got up and stood as tall as possible, walking by other guys exactly my size doing the exact same thing, and into a doctors office.

The nurse did the normal tap-the-knee type shit and checked my blood pressure. When she was done, she said I needed to head to the bathroom for my drug test.

"For sure. Where do I find the cup?"

"They'll have one for you."

They?

When I got to the bathroom there was a doctor looking man (I only assume because he was white and older and we were in a clinic... no one had coats on), and team trainer. I looked at the 'cups.' These were not dixie piss cups as I knew them. These reminded me of a situation where Tupperware made contact with The High Evolutionary. These were overgrown. They had multistep locks and all kinds of ratchets.

The trainer handed me a sheet of barcodes with medical information, and a tablet with some similar information on it. I looked at both.

"Are those numbers the same?" He asked.

Oh. I didn't see those.

"Yep."

I waited while the doctors moved barcodes and sticky tape and placed them different cups and charts like a family of nine trying to self tag their luggage.

The doctor eventually waved for me to come near. I guess everything was a go. He handed me one of the cups and held up another and again asked me to confirm the numbers. After that, he told me to pull my pants all the way down and take my shirt off.

Oh hell naww. That's full Toblerone. No fucking way.

"Uh. Ok," I said, doing both like a robot.

"Do a spin," he commanded.

"A spin?"

"A spin."

I did a spin. He told me to now urinate in the cup, but what he failed to realize was that it was now awkward. I couldn't go. I tried for what felt like forever, while the trainer flushed the toilet next to me, hoping it would get me going. It didn't.

"Do this often?" I asked to cut the tension.

"What do you mean?" The doctor replied.

"Well I'm just thinking, you gotta do all of us today. Do you just do this as a one off or do you travel around day to day, administering tests?"

"Oh. I guess, yea I am a test administrator. I'm with the testing company," the doctor turned 'just a tester guy' said, "I run tests pretty much every day of the week."

THIS GUY HAS SEEN SO MUCH DICK.

"Wow. You've seen a lot! Anything interesting?"

"I tested the Spurs a few days ago. That was pretty cool," random test guy answered.

THIS RANDOM MAN HAS SEEN TIM DUNCAN'S DICK!

"Wow! That's fascinating," I said, as I turned around and filled up the cup.

As we were reading the numbers and confirming all the science again, I had to ask why the process was so much more invasive than when I was in college.

"The Wizzonator," dude who got a job testing urine said. "Oh, and Lance Armstrong."

TRAIN HARD.

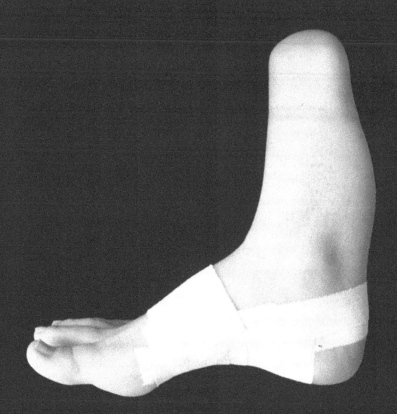

What do you want to be when you grow up? An NBA Star!

What do you want to be when you've grown up? Hey I don't want to lead you here, but you could be a trainer!

It's super dope!

Both the players and staff respect you and your time, like so much. You'll love how they only ask you to do your job which is taping! Get that tape and OMG you can suck air from the Ice bags like a pro!

If you're lucky, you can administer a drug test and get NBA urine on your hands!

DD
DIFFERENT
DUDE™

RUN IT

Summer League 2008, I was with the Toronto Raptors. It was unfortunate because I had a real shot to make the team, then I sprained my MCL late in practice on the very first day in Las Vegas. Ass, I tell you.

What was funny to me was that after practice, one of the ops assistants was helping get shit from the random Henderson, NV high school we practiced at, onto the bus. This process was not fun for him because it was July and the temperature was upwards of 108 degrees. I could tell this kid was struggling.

I guess everyone else could tell he was struggling, too. Some of the other players stopped him and interrupted his work.

"It's too hot out for you to be doing all that," someone said.

"Yea. But you know how it goes," the kid replied.

"They pay you enough for this shit?"

"You know they don't," the kid said with a smirk as he scanned the group for someone who could fire him. There weren't any of those people there.

"Shit. I'll give you $100 right now to sprint to the end of the football field and back. But you gotta go right now," the teammate continued.

"I'll add $100 to that, too," someone else chimed in.

When the dust settled, the kid had $700 in incentive to drop what he was doing and sprint 250 yards in 108 degrees. Of course he said yes, not so much because of the money, but because he was still a fan of the guys who were paying him to do this. The story was bigger than the cash. I understood at that moment that those guys knew the power they had. Money and fandom is a powerful combination.

The kid dropped what he was doing and ran the sprint. When he got back, he pretended he was totally fine, but he was dying of many ailments, heat exhaustion at the top of the list.

"Anything else?" he asked when he got back.

Kids are stupid.

NEVER PAID

My senior year of college, my character in the NCAA March Madness 2006 video game was skilled as hell. He had like 90 speed, 99 offensive rebounding, and 88 block rating. He was also white. It was a weird accident considering EA Sports was just a few miles from campus.

I never played as that man. I was also never paid.

RETINA QUALITY

When I was in Korea, late into my career, we would board the team bus after games to hit the road home. Most times these would be four hour rides that started after we had finished a hurried dinner on the floor of some soup restaurant. Tei would order me a dry pizza from Papa Johns or something and I would eat it alongside my teammates, not really speaking, especially after a loss. I can not tell you how many times I ate dry pizza and washed it down with a Chilsung.

We would then get onto the bus and everyone would settle into their routines. For me, it was a bottle of Soju tucked away under my seat, some soft emotional music, and the hope that Sharon was awake to text with me. It was all about decompression. But that's not how it always was.

In the early years, we were winning so often that a lot of the bus rides were like celebrations. I would walk up and down the aisles, cracking jokes and being stupid. There was something light about winning that made those rides feel even more youthful than they actually were.

One thing everyone would do was look at my instagram. I was the party guy in LA and the Koreans were enamored with the lifestyle that came with it. Instagram wasn't available to these guys either, so even the sight of white women at a party was unusual. They would literally gasp while scrolling through photos of people that I wouldn't look at twice. Oddly it was rewarding.

It would go something like this:

"Girlfriend?"

"No," I would reply laughing.

"Friend?"

"No."

"Sex partner?" (pronounced sechi patuna)

"I wish."

"Naked picture?"

"What man? No, I don't know her."

One day, after they saw me going through my IG page, I felt compelled to lean over and see what some of them were looking at on their phones. One of them was looking at a picture that was clearly of his girlfriend. I thought it would be funny to ask the same questions.

"Girlfriend?" I asked.

"Yes. My girlfriend," he replied quickly.

"Naked photo?"

I knew 100% without a doubt that he would NEVER show me (or anyone else) naked photos of his girlfriend, so I could continually ask him, knowing he would ju–

"Ok. Ok. One sec."

Huh? No way. I don't believe it.

"No, no. Stop!"

I was trying to communicate to him that I didn't actually want to see his girl naked and that he had successfully called my bluff.

He tossed his phone into my lap. I closed my eyes, but he kept tapping me to look.

When in Rome, right?

I squeaked open an eye and jumped back in my seat as I threw the phone back at him. It was a fully naked picture. I was shocked. I was appalled. I was disgusted because it was a picture of my other teammate who was sitting right next to him!

"Fuck! What the fuck?" I knew he knew those words.

He began to laugh uncontrollably. He proceeded to scroll through and try to get me to look at tons of fully naked photos of all my Korean teammates. I was catching full glimpses of D and B in the corner of my eye as I kept trying to avert my gaze from his phone while he waved it in front of me.

It was at this point that four other guys realized what was happening and proceeded to show me naked pictures of the first guy. There were digital versions of bush and hole everywhere around me. How could they all have SO MANY pictures of each other? I had to call over to the translator across the room for the real answers.

"Chris!" I called him and he began walking over.

"You know that these dudes all have nude pictures of one another? No hate, but is it a gay thing? Am I missing something?"

My teammate also knows the word gay and responded before Chris could.

"No gay! No gay!"

I felt bad about making him feel like I was calling him out.

"Chris, tell him I'm not trippin at all if that's how they get down. But to date I have not known a man that has naked pictures of 12 other men on their retina resolution phone. Nobody is supposed to have that much definition."

Chris translated what I said to my teammates:

"Ro-du hypo eehud sjJSHj skjsdhdhs gay gay skhdsh gay gay photo hssuskjsh."

They replied defensively:

"No! No! Gay djdhjks dhdus dsksaiuapopsomcnvas sjhb sdkjhih no gay kzldfspfsohfs photo qbajkkjiytwre plcm gay!!!"

Chris turned back to me.

"He says that it's just blackmail. They're not gay, but if they catch each other without clothes on, they take a picture to use against one another later. They're kinda doing it right now as they're embarrassing each other by showing the photos to you."

That was the last time I checked a Korean teammates camera roll.

LDS

When I was around 12, I was starting to flirt with the rim a little bit. I couldn't jump and touch it, but I was trying every damn day. It was my only mission. The church we attended, North Coast Presbyterian (yea it's a white as it sounds), had hoops in the main auditorium, so every week after church, I'd put the hoops down, get a running start on the carpeted floor, and try to touch that bad boy.

My mom, in a rare moment of sports encouragement, saw me doing this one day. She offered me a bargain: the day I could touch the rim, she'd pay me $15, and the day I could dunk, there would be $100 waiting for me. We were so broke that I didn't really believe it, but it was enough to give me the motivation I needed.

It wasn't but a few months later that I touched the rim. Sure enough, my mom found $15 and paid. Since I was now rich, I lost the drive. I stopped trying to go higher. I was too busy buying shit. I was still at an age where handing me $15 made me feel like I was capable of anything.

The next week, broke again and in need of more cash, I was back on the grind. I was trying desperately to go higher, but there was a big jump (pun intended) between touching the rim and actually dunking it. I never gave up, but it couldn't be a daily mission until my anatomy updated. I had to wait.

By the start of my sophomore year, I was close. So, so close. I could almost palm a ball, and I could hang on the rim whenever I wanted. I just couldn't get the damn ball to stay in my hands long enough to convert a dunk. I wasn't going to let that stop me, however, because I needed that hundo.

On occasion, the Torrey Pines basketball team would practice at the Mormon Church across the street. Technically, it was the church of Jesus Christ of Latter Day Saints, and technically the church had low rims. But everyone called it the Mormon Church and we all tried to dunk there. Everyone knew that the Mormon church rims were suspiciously low, so we all went there to test our abilities. This was where I tried to dunk the most often. If it was going down, it was going down there first.

One day after practice (I was on the JV team but I didn't have a jersey, so was I?) I lined up the jump and tried again. On the very first try, I dunked it. My teammates and I were both shook. Dunking felt like I had opened up an entirely new sandbox no one else was allowed to play in. I wasn't well liked and I didn't even have a jersey but I was the only one who could dunk on the team. The dunk was really all I had. That was enough for a while.

I went home and told my mom. I'd truly like to know what she was thinking when I told her the news. Again, we didn't have money. I don't know if she earmarked that hundo a couple years earlier, but I can't imagine it was just laying around. I wonder if she thought she had more time? Or was she just happy for me? Even the fact that I was considering all these things shows that we really didn't have it.

"Show me," my mom said plainly.

We got in the car right away and drove to the church. There were no less than 50 gyms between our house and the Mormon Church, but all 50 of them required an inch or two more vertical jumping ability. So we pulled up to the LDS church and went in to witness a miracle.

I didn't even need to warm up. I just grabbed the ball and went and dunked it. My mom did an impressed nod and handed me a hundred dollars. I couldn't believe she fell for it! The rim was low! Ha! Sucker!

The next day, I felt bad for having gamed the system. I spent the money, don't get me wrong, but how I got it felt bad. Not to mention that at a school like Torrey Pines, there aren't many dunkers, so word was spreading about what I'd done – and that I had done it at the Mormon Church. No one respected it.

So that very next day after practice, with the entire JV and Varsity teams watching, I lined up and dunked it again in our own gym. It was a legit ten foot dunk. That settled it. I was now a dunk man and I could spend the money with no caveats.

What's crazy is that within a few weeks, I could dunk with two hands and a few weeks after that, I could pretty much do anything. The growth process happens when it happens.

BAD GAGGLE

In the summer of 2012, I was out here doing it. We had lost in the chip, but between my salary and bonuses, I made around half a milly. Child's play for many folks age 40, but at 25 (before inflation), I essentially was a trillionaire.

When I arrived back in LA, I did a lot of rich guy shit like buy a Fisker and fly girls I liked to Vegas. I had earned the right, paying my dues in a dark room in Korea for the right to stunt in the summer. What a wild time.

Even with all that spending, I didn't really buy bottles often. I say *really* because it's all relative. I probably bought bottles ten times out of the hundred they tried to get me to buy. Them's good numbers as it pertains to drunk decision making.

One night, we got word that there was something spicy going on at The LeBrondrian hotel. It's formally known as The Mondrian, but in 2012, much like LeBron, it was the greatest on earth. If we got the call that something was going down at The LeBrondrian, we were going for sure.

When we got there, there was a long line. The doorman at the front was not in the mindset to let us in. I should mention that once you do buy bottles, you have to convince promoters to let you into shit for free for the rest of your days. Quite often we would show up somewhere and all the homies would walk right in and the promoter would stop only me, as if to remind me that with great power comes great responsibility.

Anyways, the guy was not having it, but I was trying to push and work it out. My homie John who had rolled with me was up in arms about the whole ordeal. He was very drunk, mind you, but he was being a bit performative. There is something special about the bravado of a drunk white dude that alerts an entire group that there is no problem he can't solve. It's often said in the face of a problem they can't solve. I digress.

John left to go 'handle' the situation while I stayed there just standing around. This was another thing LA promoters enjoyed doing. They knew damn well they were going to let you in, but they had to leverage their power, even if for ten minutes. So I just loitered and participated in the process, until Brian Scalabrine showed up with an enormous entourage.

Man's must have been rolling 12-15 deep, all bad women. You'd be tempted to think that the Red Mamba, who was still on the Celtics at the time, had come directly from spring break and had brought Girls Gone Wild with him. Nothing shocked me at that point in my life and still, seeing Scalabrine rolling *like that* was a sight to behold.

He walked up and the door guy changed his whole fucking tune. He started dapping Brian up and I could see a twinkle in this man's eye. He was smiling ear to ear like Drake at a Kentucky basketball game. He was so excited to be near Scalabrine it damn near felt racist and the man was black.

Does this man know I'm a half millionaire?

He did. That was the point.

I caught Scalabrine's eye and motioned to him as if to signal 'you know the deal' and he confidently nodded. We played basketball long enough to recognize a brother in arms in need of help.

He knows the deal.

John came back right then and joined me in line. He was gonna say something, but I told him we were good and to shut up. We were. As soon as he was prompted, Brian Scalabrine pointed to everyone, the two of us included.

The front guy then pulled him aside and they had a pow wow. They were looking and pointing my direction and I knew something was wrong. I looked at John, and I asked him what happened when he left.

"Tried to get in. Didn't work. Look alive."

I whipped my head back towards the front. They were still debating while Red Mamba was growing increasingly frustrated. Finally, he just screamed:

"Everyone who's not blacklisted! Come with me!"

I started walking in, foolishly, and the front door man stopped both John and me. He informed me that he had already caught John trying to hop a fence and had explicitly told him he was blacklisted. Thus, by proxy, I was also blacklisted. We were turned away and I didn't even try to fight back. Only an idiot fights a blacklisting. We've all seen Night at the Roxbury.

Scalabrine kept walking with his gaggle of bad ones and didn't even look back.

Damn. He knows the deal.

CUT 4

When Larry Bird called me into his office a week into training camp, I figured it was a very overkill way to fire me. I was right. He was not there to fire me. He spent a good five minutes explaining that Jamaal Tinsely shot himself in the leg the year before and that the Malice in the Palace was still being felt socially throughout Indiana.

"We can't have any more issues here," he said matter of factly, "so while you're here, we'd prefer you don't blog."

I wasn't cut. I was just being asked to stop writing about Steak and Shake? I was confused but I stopped.

A couple weeks later, Jim O'Brien called me into his office. I knew what it was this time. For a man who spent literally every day yelling at Roy Hibbert about how much better than him I was playing, he seemed pretty sure that I wasn't going to work.

"You could have been in better shape," were the last words he ever said to me.

SAVAGE INSULTS

As college freshmen, we were brutal to one another. We would make fun of literally anything about you. Any one thing out of place and we were coming for your neck. Nothing wrong with you at all? You're too perfect. We still coming.

It got so bad one day that my Spanish teammate cried. He was learning English for the first time and, to be dicks, we started speaking hella fast and disrespectfully.

"Yourmomsucksalotofdicks."

"Hu-what-uh?" he would scramble to ask.

"Yourmomsucksalotofdicks," we would continue.

"All the day I try English and you help me no!"

We even laughed at his crying response. It was so damn mean.

Probably our most consistent insult was a kind of a "what he looks like" game. It was pretty simple. If there was a beat up looking, less attractive, or whatever older man, we would always say something like "Hey David, what's your uncle doing here?" and everyone would laugh. It was low hanging fruit for 18 year olds.

One day we were at USC finishing up shoot around in the morning. As we traded our shoes for slides and grabbed our bags to exit the old LA Sports Arena, there was a man walking near the team bus. He looked potentially unhoused, missing a couple teeth (which we could tell from hundreds of yards away), and he was tall and darker skinned. I knew what was coming.

"Rod man what's your pops doing here?!"

"Ayo why Rod's uncle look like the family withheld his funding?"

Shit was funny, not gonna lie. It was my turn and I knew the rules. Negro looked like me, so it was what it was. He looked like me so it was natural. He looked like I looked so… He looked. Like. Me. Like, exactly like me.

Wait.

Suddenly everyone stopped clowning me as they made the same realization I did: that was my *actual* dad I hadn't seen in years. I slowed up and let the guys get on the bus.

As I stared into the eyes of what I can only describe as a dilapidated version of my future self, I felt every emotion possible, save for joy.

"Hey son. How are you?" he began.

I don't remember the rest.

HARD LIQUOR AND MALICIOUS AMBITION

It was spring 2006, a week before Senior Night, and I was out at a frat party. I can't remember the name of the frat, but it was one I had been to quite a few times.

In those days, frat parties were hit and miss for me. I had only started drinking at the start of my sophomore year and I decided right away that beer was horrible. That would be fine, except fraternities seemed hellbent on providing as much beer as possible, almost like a badge of honor.

Thus, at most frat parties, I spent the majority of the time trying to find the answer to one question: where is the hard liquor? It would seem like an easy question to answer, but most nights it led me down some weird rabbit holes. I was like a 21 year-old hosting a shitty collegiate version of 'Parts Unknown.'

On this particular night, I was walking in and out of random rooms, hoping to see a brother with a bottle. As I whipped from one room to another, I came across some RallyCom kids in one of the rooms. They had liquor. Jackpot.

RallyCom, short for Rally Committee, was a student group at Cal that essentially lead the student section in hype. It was like a step below cheerleader or dancer, but way more enthused than the normal student. RallyCom kids go hard for the team, that's why I knew they'd hook a brotha up with some clear drank.

As we poured up, one of the kids turned to me. I forget his name now, so I'll call him J. J comes in HOT with a story that I'm struggling to keep up with given my level of intoxication. As he's talking, I start hearing some words that sound funny. It sounds something like

"Man… USC… Pruitt… HAHAHAHA… Check this out!"

He pulls out his sidekick and shows me some messages. I look at them and then back up at him.

"Wait. You're texting Gabe Pruitt? From U$C? But using someone else's pictures?"

"Yea!… Shirtless… Oh My God Man… Saturday!"

The next morning I was unsure if I dreamed the conversation or not, but if it was real it didn't make sense. You couldn't just send someone a message using someone else's pictures, could you? No one in their right mind would fall for that, would they? This was all a novel concept. I decided to go on living my life because the thought didn't make sense.

On March 4th, 2006, I got dressed in the locker room like any other day. I laced up my LeBrons (yea they were already hot) and threw on my headband. I put on my long sleeve warm up and left my jersey in the locker for later. I downed a gatorade shake, and I headed up the tunnel into the arena. I guess it wasn't *any* game. It was Senior Night. Win or lose, we had to win. So my focus was laser.

AYOOOOOOOOOOOO!!!!!

That's the only memory I have of what I thought when I got to the top of the tunnel. There were RallyCom students already there, holding gigantic placards with Gabe Pruitt's phone number on them. Each digit its own 36x48 inch offense.

Others had big posters covered in large shirtless photos of the USC Freshman guard. When I got all the way to the court, I could see they were also placing sheets of paper on all the seats in the arena. The sheets were printed with fully laid out conversations between Gabe and a made up woman, Victoria.

This man was getting after it in the chats. It was so damn horny. He was sending photos and asking to meet up and really making a play for this particular weekend.

What a crazy thing for me to read right before a game. It was so aggressive, I remember thinking that women must find me hella tame if they were used to that level of pressure. Regardless, I put the sheet down and got back to warm ups.

This is gonna be weird.

An elderly couple, dripped in Cal gear so old that it could have been hand stitched before The War, sat down and started reading one of the sheets.

THIS IS DEFINITELY GOING TO BE WEIRD.

When Pruitt finally walked out and saw everything, he clearly had no idea any of this was going on. HE HAD NO FUCKING IDEA WHAT WAS HAPPENING. I kid you not it was like a Catfish reveal in front of ten thousand people who hated him. He was shook. Super shook. I'd love to say he played it off, but he actually couldn't. No one had heard of catfishing. No one thought about it. He legitimately did not understand the moment until the entire crowd started chanting "VIC-TOR-IA! VIC-TOR-IA!"

'J' was leading everyone. The man had done it. I looked up at him and he waved and pointed. I looked back at Gabe and he reminded me of the meme where a man with a crying face puts on a mask of a fake smile. It was that bad.

Even though he was rattled, he still had to play in the game. This was brutal. Dude did not play well at all. It might have been the worst game of his life. Sure, we were a tournament team, and maybe we may have won anyway, but what RallyCom did to Gabe Pruitt fully took him out of the game.

Not only that, we played with so much hype considering that it was Senior Night. The entire game was like a circus and all of us, fans included, were the ringleaders. In fact, one of the walk-on seniors, Steve Panawek got a breakaway dunk and you'd think we won Wimbledon. The celebration was that crazy.

There was no way USC was going to win that game. They could hardly shoot free throws without seeing the nipples of their team captain.

It was so damn funny then, but now it feels kinda wrong. Gabe really thought he was building something for real with an actual woman. Instead it was a white frat boy who had both hard liquor and malicious ambition.

I SEE YOU PLAYER 2

The second time a woman DM'd me from the stands, I saw it coming a mile away. It was during Summer League and I was literally in the game about to shoot a free throw. I looked towards the bench to get the defensive call and there was a white woman just staring me directly in the eye a few rows up at the Cox Center.

There was no denying this. It actually threw me for a second. No one had ever looked at me like that who didn't know me.

Bro she is staring directly into your future.

When I got back to the hotel and checked MySpace, sure enough there was a DM. I checked her page and was surprised, both by how forward she was and how innocent her page was. I actually interpreted it as someone not understanding what they were talking about. Her main was her in a white polo and jeans, alongside like forty other white folks dressed the same. The location was Provo, UT. Everything else about her page was about being Mormon. Her message:

"What are you doing later?"

So, yea, I thought it was kind of a kid fan just asking about my day in general. That was not her intention. She said that she was into me and we just kind of stayed in one another's orbit, until the next time my D-League team went to Provo.

We met up at the Marriott (where else?) and had one non-alcoholic drink in the lobby bar. We then took it upstairs and proceeded to have sex in the room while my teammate in the other bed pretended to read a book.

There was a lot of that sort of thing back then. Looking back, the fact that everyone just did it and no one ever asked questions is kind of wild. To be young, I suppose.

Anyways, it was not good. Not good at all. No bueno. That's when she told me she was a virgin.

WHAT?

WATCH THE THRONE

I missed a lot being overseas for years and today I'll make it clear the event I missed the most: the Watch The Throne tour.

Today, I wouldn't give Kanye a damn dollar, but in 2011 it was a different story. This man announced a tour that started in September and ended in December, so I was gone for the whole thing. That alone was fine and happened a lot.

What was ass was that he made it a point to play "Niggas in Paris" more and more times the longer the tour went on. So I would be up, mid day in Korea, watching people update their FB news feeds with "Kanye just shut down Baltimore! He played Niggas in Paris five times!"

This continued all damn fall and he ended the tour in LA. This was especially difficult because he was playing the song nine and ten times to close out the shows and all I could do was read about it from every person I knew.

This was the first time I realized that being able to afford something but not having the time for it felt worse than not having the option at all. One of many lessons learned in the darkness of my Korean apartment.

NEON BLACK

In 2018, after I retired, everyone had unsolicited input about what I should do going forward. I already knew what I was going to do. I previously met with a producer at Fox Sports in 2015 who invited me to the lot to meet other producers. He remembered me from Yahoo! and told me that when I was done, they would be waiting.

But I hadn't heard back from him… Since 2017. So the suggestions kept coming in while I waited for a reply from Fox. My guy Brandon Sutton suggested I do Improv.

"Improv?"

"Yea. On stage and all that," he said, sounding more creole than normal.

"Why?"

"No reason. I just dare you."

A week later and I was in Improv 101. This was a very 'Yes Man' phase of my life.

Coincidentally, Mother's Day was just around the corner. Any good son knows that when a mom drops an obvious context clue, you don't ignore it. Months beforehand, my mom bought me a kids watercolor set.

"You used to be so good at art."

Whatever you say, mom. Watercolors are for children.

I made her a painting as a gift. It wasn't particularly good, but it was a portrait of Whitney Houston, done with stencils in a Banksy-like fashion. She loved it so much that I felt compelled to share on Instagram. That's when the 'be an artist' suggestions started flying in.

I hated all of these suggestions. I didn't connect with the notion of being an artist. Artists lived lives that I didn't lead. They were emotional and could access feelings I couldn't. Most importantly, they felt compelled to paint. I did not.

I reached peak annoyed-ness while in San Francisco for Bay to Breakers. Sharon and Nico were talking past me discussing details of an art show I didn't plan on having.

"I can set up the DJ Booth, I have some connections," he said.

"Well if it's going to be a September opening, that should give us enough time to make adjustments," she replied. She was both very good at this type of thing and very into it.

"Stop. There isn't going to be a show!" I declared, hoping they'd believe me. They didn't. Fake plans kept happening around me.

That July, I was in Las Vegas for the summer league. Dongbu and I had been in conversations for me to become a scout with them in retirement. If Fox Sports was going to keep taking their time, I had to start becoming responsible and get that income going. So I met with the Koreans for dinner at the MGM. They were delighted to see me, even though I was getting fat.

"It's nice to see you, Benson. You are fat now," the head coach said.

When I left dinner, we had a handshake deal. I would begin working for them, starting this trip, helping them scout summer league for talent and then continuing throughout the season.

I got back to my room at the Wynn and checked my phone. My boy Brandon Turner was coming into town and I hadn't seen him in years. He wanted to go out to OMNIA at Caesars to catch up. I was into it, seeing as I was celebrating a new job.

When I got to OMNIA, it was a total shit show. I hadn't been to a club during summer league in years. I liked it less. Summer league had become a way bigger production since 2010, and people everywhere were gravitating towards me like I was someone important. The crowd around us was so thick that I literally had to move people out of the way every time we wanted to relocate, which was often because the walk from the entrance of OMNIA to the dance floor is a mile.

When we were making our final descent into the main dance floor, I guess I swam the wrong guy. I remember him looking up briefly, angered, but I can't remember his face. I wish I did. The next thing I know, I was lifted up off the ground. One man had my legs and another had my torso, secured by my neck. I couldn't make a sound. It happened so swiftly that Brandon and them didn't even know I was gone.

I was taken to a dark room in the back. Honestly, it was exactly what you see in movies when Joe Pesci is about to break someone's legs. They laid me face down and handcuffed me. I could finally talk. Instead, I screamed.

"What the fuck is this?! What's happening?"

"Sir, we need you to calm down."

Oh. It's one of these.

"Excuse me, what have I done wrong?"

They didn't answer. The swept man walked in, took a seat 15 feet in front of me and crossed his legs. They were all I could see without straining. It's part of the reason I don't remember his face. I could see it only with a painful contortion of my neck. He was smiling, though. I knew that much.

"We can't let you go until this man decides if he wants to press charges," I thought I heard security say. It was still loud back there. The walls did nothing to stop the bass of a Kaskade Residency.

I was getting drunk, too. I hate that I have to say that but I have to say that. I went out to a party in Vegas to celebrate a new job. My drunkenness was rising as I was laying there, handcuffed and confused.

"I hate to say this, but can you get me the police?" I asked, feeling bad for the brotha of the two security guards.

They flashed their badges. They were the police.

They kept me there while this man sat, smiling, waiting for me to break. And I knew he wanted that, too. Everytime I looked up, squirming to make eye contact, he just smirked and smiled, knowing damn well there were no charges to press.

I did break. It took an hour, but I broke down into full tears. It's funny, I don't think the tears were just for my pain at that moment. Part of me was so distraught that people want to behave that way to other people. To me. That this black man sat there with a knee on my back the whole time, awaiting his orders, knowing his paycheck had long since become a larger priority than his scrutinous eye.

But I was most distraught that they got to see the real me. They saw the me nobody gets to see; the powerless version. No amount of size, strength, education, intelligence, resume, dunks, contact list, or anything mattered. I was just bare.

Once it was clear I was beneath them, they threw me out onto the street. It was some place I didn't recognize. My clothes were all covered in dirt and damp with tears. I finally got to look at my phone. I had something like 200 missed calls and texts, some from Brandon, confused thinking I ditched him and asking what he did wrong. There were more from Sharon, assuming I was up to no good, and even more from friends in LA thinking she was up to no good. It was all a lot.

The next morning, I locked myself in my hotel room and did what I did best. I drank myself numb, crying pools of tears I didn't know were possible. I changed my flight. I couldn't stay in Las Vegas any longer. The next available flight I could get was for the following morning, so I just kept drinking until I blacked out.

When I got back to LA, there were three huge canvases leaning against the front door of my loft. I looked at the receipt, confused. They were for me. I took them inside and checked my email. I'd ordered them while I was blacked out.

Why the hell would I do that?

The return fee was crazy high, seeing how big they were, so I just kept them. After a few days of staring at these giant white obstructions, I felt compelled to paint a kneeling Colin Kaepernick. It was done in the same style as the Whitney I did for my mother.

This also was not good. It was too colorful. Too colorful, indeed, but I liked it. I liked neon shit. Why was it always so bad to like neon shit? I realized I was painting myself, in a way. My shade of black *was* neon. I was Neon Black.

I decided I would have an art show, if only to show the world that Neon Black existed. So I started planning. It was all I could do, now that I left the Koreans unanswered in Las Vegas and lost that opportunity. Fox wasn't calling. It was like the universe was forcing me to be an artist against my will, but it happened.

I opened Neon Black, my first solo show, in Hollywood on September 28th, 2018.

Sharon was right. Everyone was right.

PRAY ON IT

At an AAU tournament in 2001, my teammates cornered me in a Vegas hotel room and threw a bible at me. When I caught it, they quickly asked if I ever masturbated. Feeling like Jesus was watching me, I reluctantly said that had. The laughter was thunderous.

I'm still unsure if 'no' was a better answer.

MIKE FUCKING BIBBY

The summer of 2006 was full of tumult. I had recently graduated from Berkeley and was asked to enter "the real world," but I had no funds. Everything was dramatic as a result, especially in Sacramento because I had never been and was struggling.

Sac wasn't just a new city. It was super specific. It seemed like a place where each of its specific areas was always highlighted as being different. Each area had its people, events, theaters, etc. The only people who seemed to operate with no limits and cross all these imaginary boundaries were the Sacramento Kings.

The Kings ran the city of Sacramento. It almost felt like you weren't even allowed to have fun in the entire county without King's approval. I could say that I was going to a bar.

"Oh the one Bobby Jackson be at?"

"No. What?"

"You trippin."

If the Kings were not doing it, it was pointless.

There was this time we were leaving a bar and this dude kept telling everyone that there was an after party at Kevin Martin's house. He had all of us into it. We offered to drive him there, just so we wouldn't miss out. When we got there, Kevin wasn't there. No one was. Dude chunked up the deuces and went to sleep. We drove an hour the wrong way for no reason. This was the Sacramento I knew.

No one ran the city more, in a specific way, than Team Dime. Team Dime was just Mike Bibby and his nine homies from Arizona, but they were EVERYWHERE. We'd be at the club, and TD would be in the building doing it bigger. Always. I actually thought they were just swole ass club promoters, but they were more than that.

I found out what Team Dime really does one day when someone walked into the gym we were training out of, and said there was an open run at another spot. He asked if I wanted to get down.

"Sure," I said, "game don't stop."

When the dude left, someone else pulled me aside.

"Yo Bro, You don't wanna go play out there. Team Dime is gonna be there."

"Team Dime? The promoters?"

"What?"

"What?"

"I don't know what you're talking about but yea they be at the club. You don't wanna play pickup with them."

He never really explained why, so I didn't take it seriously. I headed out to the other run to get some work in. As I was changing into my kicks, I watched the run. It only took 30 seconds of watching to understand why I was warned. These dudes looked much more swole in basketball shit than in Ed Hardy, and they used 100% of that swoleness to foul the shit out of the other team. Bibby was very good. He's Mike fucking Bibby. But the other guys played like some other guys.

The other, better team could have still won, but when they got close, the fouls started going crazy. When they got upset and seemed ready to scrap, the other half of Team Dime sitting in the stands would stand up as if to say 'don't even try it.'

To my knowledge, TD has never lost a game because this formula is extraordinarily effective. By combining the King's social power, Mike Bibby's skill, and 10 swole dudes who seemed ready to do a bid at a moments notice, Team Dime had constructed pickup basketball immortality.

To this day, I don't think they have ever lost.

EMAILS FROM BILL 5

* From: —--@hanmail.net

* To: BILL

* Sent: 7/28/2010 10:36:12 P.M. Eastern Daylight Time

* Subj: Hi this is Dongbu Basketball team

* * *

Hi I'm Tei from Dongbu Basketball team. we are also happy to work with Rodrigue Benson. I'm his translater for this season so pls contact me anything about Rod. And pls tell him that he should start work out for season because its really going to be hard for preparing season when he come to Korea And I need copy of his passport as quick as possible for reservation flight Thanx lets keep in touch

IT WAS THE WORK

The second time I retired, it was much less glamorous. I was retired for a year and a half when my money started looking weird. There was a combination of not exactly knowing how to be a professional at anything else and a deal I thought I had at Fox Sports that fell through, leaving me in a position where I was considering the quickest fix I knew.

I got the call to do 3X3 Jeddah Masters in Saudi Arabia from some of my old friends in Korea looking for a ringer. I figured it would be hella easy because it was 3X3 (not real basketball) plus the purse was high enough that I should figure to bring back enough money to solve all my problems. Forever.

The first thing I didn't consider was that Sharon would not like this plan one bit. I was so used to packing up and making choices that only affected myself. After a year and a half of being retired, the notion that I would just pick up and go back to Asia for a month was wild to her, but not to me. My basketball mind kicked in and the civilian mind shut off. We were not on good terms when I left for that trip, but I needed the cash.

Before I got to the Jeddah Masters, there were a couple of Korean tournaments leading in. Each of them had big purses for the winners, upwards of $40k, so we were highly motivated. I need to say the cash amount because I do think people assume we are playing basketball for the love of the game. Some people are, but it's far fewer than those who won't lace up if their check isn't on time. Most guys are all about the money or some version of it, anyway. Myself included after so many years.

The first tournament was literally inside of a shopping mall. Lotte Tower, to be exact, one of the tallest buildings in the world. But the ground floor was just another excuse to have a Louis Vuitton store in the middle of a theme park. Part of the attraction that day was us, team "Musso," playing on a makeshift sport court stadium, complete with digital marquees and screens everywhere. It was not a small production.

It was me, Eric and Daniel Sandrin, and a Korean point guard whose name I forget. The Sandrins are half-Korean half-American brothers who were some of the most famous basketball players in the country. They were the ones who called me to come play because they remembered my game from the KBL.

The hype was that these guys were trying to qualify for the Olympics and they needed a certain amount of points in various tournaments to do so. I didn't know that until I got there. I was just going for the money. But because of this extra motivation, these guys were playing for the pride of their country. I was not.

Since I didn't respect 3X3 players at all, I had no idea of the stakes. We won some and lost some. I was very overweight and out of shape, but I was still better than these yokels. We took 4th, and upon claiming that spot, a Korean team had its best finish ever. Daniel ran up to chest bump me and he missed because I didn't jump.

"Man! Celebrate! This is huge!" he pleaded.

I just didn't have the same hype. It's like Jokic in the NBA finals. I didn't learn the value of those games the same as they did, so there was nothing to celebrate. 4th only came with a $2k prize. That wasn't going to do it.

The second tournament, held on Jeju Island, went worse. We were tired. The games were outdoors in the wind, which was an excuse I could use after missing so many shots. It was not fun. There was no money earned. We decided that the Korean PG wasn't going to get it done, so we called my guy Sheldon Bailey.

Sheldon is known for being LeBron James body double for the last decade. He also played high level basketball overseas and in college. At the time, he was playing in the Venice Beach league and staying in shape. I had so little respect for the talent level of 3X3 that I knew Sheldon would be unguardable if he was at all in shape and ready to go. He arrived in Seoul with a week before the big tournament and we got to work, planning our strategy for Saudi.

We flew into Jeddah from Seoul and that was a weird fight. The plane was completely empty save for us and a couple other folks, but it was a Boeing 777. It was massive. I had an entire section of the Saudi Air plane to myself, so I laid out and made a blanket fort.

We landed at a small airport, flying over Mecca just at sunrise on the way in. When we deplaned, we walked into the customs area and it was completely overstaffed. There must have been 200 people working the customs desks, all women, covered head to toe in black. I have been to a lot of places and seen a lot of things, but it had been a while since I truly *felt* how different a place was before I got through customs.

When we arrived at the hotel, it was essentially a military bunker in the middle of the desert. There were these gigantic spikes coming from the ground that had to be lowered for the van to even enter the premises. But once we were inside, it was amazing. The food was good. The rooms were nice. I've found that when I go to countries with less confidence from American travelers, they OD on making sure we're comfortable. They want us to go home talking about how great the country is. It's always a lie, but it's always so nice.

Our games were scheduled for 1 a.m. because it was so hot in Jeddah, so I spent most of the next day laying around waiting for them to feed us. Not Sheldon. He started getting dressed out of nowhere.

"Where are you going?" I asked knowing there was nowhere to go.

"I got a date," he replied matter of factly.

After the bewilderment settled, he explained himself.

"Someone sent a message to me DM's. I'm about to head out."

Simple as that.

In Saudi Arabia in 2019, a 'date' meant he was going to go on a very long, public walk. The laws had just opened up so that women could drive and be out in public and a whole host of things that you would assume were given rights. So it was kind of a big deal that they went and walked along the Red Sea, discussing who knows what. They really did take a risk.

When it was game time, I could see in Sheldon's eyes that he was already exhausted. We all were, to be fair, between the travel and the unbearable heat, but only one of us had gone on a 6 hour walk that day.

From the first play of the first game, Sheldon was not himself. He got burned on a back cut for an easy layup and looked around confused. We have the footage. After that, we essentially got destroyed. It's kind of funny if I don't think about all the money we lost.

I do also think that I underestimated the level of play. The Korean mall was one thing. The Jeddah masters was another. These dudes were good. I was still one of the better players there, but so what? I was scoring 1's and they were scoring 2's. It was so tiring that I was ineffective, even if I had been in shape.

I want to say Sheldon saved the day, but he did not. In fact, by replacing a Korean with him, the Korean media was unkind to the Sandrins, accusing them of not supporting their country. It was BS.

After we got our asses handed to us by every country formerly part of the Soviet Union, I realized I wasn't built for this anymore. It wasn't the talent, it was the work. It was the uncertainty of pay. It was the fact that I had to pick up and leave at a moment's notice, further fracturing my relationship. And I came home with absolutely zero money. I was never even paid my share of the $2000 pot.

All of that, and I was back where I started, just with a more fed up significant other. I gave up basketball because it could no longer quickly solve my problems.

NO MORE LOCKED DOORS

I don't care where or when, if you played college basketball, you had a few weed heads on your squad. My team was no exception. Jerry, Sean, and Terrance were our guys. They were always either going to or coming from smoking weed. They always smelled like it and their eyes were always red. If their smoking was a secret, it was a poorly kept one. Still, it was a kept one.

I actually never understood how these guys avoided getting busted in the drug test game, cause I was tested multiple times a year and sometimes I'd be scared I might get a positive result just from kicking it in their vicinity. Still, positive test or nah, they were somehow always in trouble for smoking weed. Admittedly, I knew nothing about weed save for what they told us on commercials, which I believed: "tHIS IS YOur BraIN ON DruGS"

For these guys, I would always have the same two questions:

How can you play high?

Why can't you stop?

Now that I'm a weed head myself, the answer to both questions is 'yes.' Back then however, they seemed like questions that always needed to be answered, because the guys were constantly in trouble for it.

The coaches were savages about it, too. They'd bring me in alone and try to get me to snitch on all the weed activities. I actually didn't know enough about weed or their movements to say much. Even if I did snitch, which I can't remember, I can remember thinking that I was only being asked because everyone knew what was going on. Why even get me to say anything if it wasn't a known issue? I didn't feel I was adding any intel, but have the coaches tell it we were on a mission to save these young men's lives.

Anyways, this was the cycle for years. They would get into trouble and we'd have to do conditioning as a team or do some sort of punishment to atone for their sins. We all ran for each other's sins, but this level of punishment was unique to them.

One day I was over at Jerry's house, (we always kicked it there because he had the PS2 and Madden) and of course the three wise men were getting blazed mid day. At this time, Jerry had a very strict rule about locking the doors because he was out here getting it in sexually, and he didn't know who might show up demanding answers.

To me, this was the funniest shit ever, especially since he lived in a house with upwards of nine points of entry and multiple non-athlete roommates. He literally lived with some 30 year old man who came and went at all hours. Jerry attempting to block all these points of entry all the time was an undertaking, to say the least.

That day, we were posted in the room when there was a knock on the bedroom door. This meant that one of the entry points had been breached, because no one knocked on the bedroom door without first knocking on the front door. I immediately picked up on this and whipped the door open, expecting to see one of Jerry's lady friends standing there upset because he didn't answer a text. Instead, our assistant coach was standing there looking all of us in the eye while the guys were all holding blunts.

No joke, they were all kicked off the team shortly after. Being caught red handed was a new level, even for them. The staff was already looking to do something about them, and I handed them everything they needed to execute. To this day, I'm unsure if they think I set them up or not, but I still wish it had just been a girl standing there and not Coach, but that was what it was.

BONUS

A week or so later, I was trying to convince Jerry to come in and plead his case to get back on the team. He had no interest. We got into an argument because he was hell bent on driving down to LA for a Laker game. If he wasn't going to be on the team, he may as well go see Kobe on some free tickets. I gave up and told him to have fun at the game.

THAT GAME WAS KOBE'S 81 POINT GAME.

COACH.

Feel like your career is coming to an end?

Probably so, if you played professional or collegiate basketball.

Luckily there's a career path with so much opportunity -- you can coach!

Don't know X's and O's? Never led a team? Were you really even that good? No one cares at all! All you need is a double breasted suit with five buttons on the jacket.

Keep your players in line, win those games, deal with the media, sign that star player, lose your job if it goes poorly, live a better life!

DD
DIFFERENT
DUDE™

SILVER

In the summer of 2008, I was training in Sacramento and staying in a big house funded by Bill that included a few other players. I would go work out in the mornings at the gym, then rush back home to catch the Olympics. That was because I had multiple friends competing.

I'd sit in this very 70's style living room, eating Hamburger Helper (real G's move in silence like lasagna), thinking about how crazy it was that I knew them. Some of them brought back medals that I still brag about to this day.

That was the first time I realized we, as athletes, were doing truly amazing shit. I felt happy for the homies, but also for myself. Life was about to get more interesting.

MCDONALDS AT SUNRISE

In my D-League years, I got into blackjack. It started when I lived in North Dakota because, for some reason, most bars in Bismarck had a blackjack table inside with low limits and even single decks at times. At a certain point during my rookie season, taking after a couple of vets, I started playing $1 hands.

I figured my strategy out quickly, which was to literally quit the moment I won two hands or lost what I wanted to bet. Eventually I got decent at it and would often go home up $8 or so. It wasn't big or anything, but I started to really look forward to taking home a couple extra bucks. At this time I was making maybe $400 every two weeks, so yea every dollar counted.

My next D-league stop was Reno, and the blackjack was now everywhere because of Nevada law. I had some teammates coming into practice bragging about winning $800, $3000, etc. on a daily basis. I knew I didn't have the means to play like that, but eventually I did occasionally start playing some low stakes games at the back of the El Dorado after our games. It wasn't as frequent as in Bismarck, but it was frequent enough that I stayed sharp.

In Reno, I'd mostly win, bringing home around $50-$75 in winnings most nights. There would be nights I'd come home down a bit, too, but there were more wins than losses.

Fast forward a couple months to the Summer of 2009 when I played for the Houston Rockets in the NBA Summer League in Las Vegas. We checked into the Golden Nugget (right?) in Downtown and were handed our room keys and our envelopes.

The envelopes contained our per diem which was the most important part of summer league to a broke D-Leaguer like myself. No joke, the $1,100 I would get for summer league per diem was equal to 18% of my total salary for the year, and the only amount that was tax free. Cash, baby.

I think that staying at the Golden Nugget had a lot to do with what followed because it had lower limits and tables with less restrictions. It's the Golden Nugget, after all. So I grabbed $100 from my envelope and designated this to be my gambling budget for the week. If I lost it all on the first day, I would quit and move on.

The first hand I played was poolside at the Golden Nugget. I played for about twenty minutes and by the end of that 20 minutes of playing I was up to $220. That was it for the day. The next day, it was the same thing. I took out $100 and at the end of playing, I had $175. Repeating this process through the week and half we were there, I had about $700 in winnings. It felt like Christmas in July.

On the last game day, I finally had a late night out because our summer league games were now over. I went out to the newly opened XS at Encore and realized that this was the first club I had been to that had blackjack tables inside. Genius. I sat down and played a few hands. Mind you this is a Wynn property so the minimums there were $100 after midnight. I still walked away from XS up another $100.

That walk took me back out through the main tables of the Encore where I decided to sit down again and play one last hand on my way out of Las Vegas. I put down $100, as it was the minimum bet. I hit 11, doubled down, and black jack. It was crazy. I decided to play a few more hands because this was a hot table and all the high rollers playing alongside me were winning too.

I can not lie when I say the next hour is a drunken blur, but what I know for sure is that I just kept winning. I found myself with $11,000 in chips. 11 KAY, BRO. I announced to all my new best friends at the table that this next hand would be my last hand. I put $5500 in my pocket and bet the rest. YOLO amirite?

Anyways, I got dealt an 11 and the dealer was showing 5. You don't get to this point not playing the numbers, so I doubled down. I didn't just double down, I stared into the faces of all the fifty year old white men around me, wearing suits, and toting models like bags, making $60000 bets and asked for advice. LIKE AN IDIOT. They, of course, said to do it.

She dealt me a 4 and dealt herself a jack and a 6 and took ALL MY MONEY. ALL OF IT.

After my chest allowed me to breathe again, I composed myself and thought about it.

I know the formula. I just won 20 hands in a row and literally lost just once. I can do it again. I can do it again, for sure.

So I went to the ATM and withdrew $100.

I think it was on the 5th attempt to withdraw money on a credit advance that my bank called me and essentially told me I was going into debt and to stop. I lost so many times and kept trying to dig myself out of the hole. Now I was $3200 in the red including the per diem. I looked up from the ATM, crack red eyes, alone, broke as ever, and I walked out of the hotel. I could hear the Great Gatsby-esque sounds of the real estate dudes and their winnings fading as I stepped onto Las Vegas BLVD. The sun was fully out and it hurt my eyes to open them, but it hurt my soul more knowing I must have been gambling for eight hours.

I walked across the street to McDonalds and bought an Egg McMuffin with my last $5 and I haven't gambled since.

CUT 5

I was out at a bar in Korea in 2014 doing my thang when Reggie Okosa walked in. Reggie was a fantastic basketball player who had experience in Korea before I arrived. He shouldn't have just been loitering around a bar in Korea since he wasn't under contract with anyone. No one just *is* in a country they haven't signed in.

"I just wanna let you know you should watch your back, Rod. They talking about you," he warned.

"Let 'em talk," I said back defiantly.

I was cut the next day. He was there on a tryout for my spot.

CONFUSING SEXUAL NATURE

The year was 2004 and us Cal Bears had just played the University of Washington in Seattle on New Year's Eve. We lost that game by close to 15 points because Washington was just much better than us at the time, but we didn't care (more than necessary) because it was New Year's Eve.

Obviously we were hoping to find a party on the streets of downtown Seattle, but the immediate problem was that most of us (including myself) were not 21. In fact, on that particular team, we had no seniors so only one person on the entire team was 21 and that was Richard Midgley. In true Richard fashion, he didn't want to come out and do anything because he took losses hard. Or at least, he took them harder than we did. So the rest of us, nary a man among us of drinking age, took a walk in hopes of finding some place we could make a memory.

The mission was made more difficult because we chose to walk and it was raining pretty heavily. It should also be noted that the streets were super dead. **I'm not saying that Seattle is boring** as I've been there since and it was fine, but at that moment it was damn near embarrassing how little was happening. Most places were closed and the ones that were open were completely empty. How could a major metro area have no obvious places to go on NYE?

What we also discovered right away was that if a place was open, it most certainly didn't allow under 21 entry. So in the era before google on phones, we were basically stuck with what we could discover in person and on that night, it seemed like that was an impossible task. That was until we saw a big sign that read "18+" and decided to see what the catch was.

When we got close, we discovered that the catch was that this was a Peep Show. I had literally no idea what a peep show even meant. I contend that most people still have no clue. I think I understood that it meant something taboo, but in the way we used to think about Playboy magazines or something. It was abstract knowledge.

We all knew it would be something weird, at least. So we thought that if we could all get in, we might as well try. I would never have imagined what was actually waiting for us when we inevitably walked in.

If you've been to a Peep Show before, none of this is going to surprise you. If you haven't, maybe you'll be as shocked as I was to find out that there was nobody working the door of this place. In fact, there was no security of any kind which was both concerning and lit. In my mind, no security also meant that even the 18+ thing might be made up. Maybe this was just a restaurant that we misunderstood. Either way, we were in the building.

There was a cash machine and an ATM right inside the front door. We studied the machine, curious as to what its use was. Via trial and error, someone figured out that it was literally just a coin exchange. He put one dollar in and got four quarters back. It was then that we noticed that we appeared to be in a staging area but there were booths nearby. It was beginning to make sense that this may be a solo experience, so we all put a dollar into the machine and found a booth.

When I sat down in my booth, I didn't know what I was looking at. It was very dark, there was a stool, and there was a quarter slot akin to what is on the front of a pinball machine. I took one of the quarters and put it in the slot. RIGHT AWAY the wall in front of my face rose up and revealed a window and a room on the other side. There was a naked lady dancing in the least engaging way. It was weird. It was like a zoo cage with a real woman inside, dancing and looking like an unsexy ghost.

What was more weird was that a second into watching this, part of the wall in the distance flew up and I could literally see my teammate, then my wall slammed back down. I rushed another quarter into the slot. My wall flew back up. Now there were walls flying up and down as we were realizing what this was. It became clear that a quarter bought literally a few seconds of time. I'd put a quarter in, my wall would go up, I'd see all the homies (many of us dancing and doing dumb shit by the third time) and then a confused looking stripper would keep working in silence as the walls would slam back down. It was certainly an experience.

We knew that if it cost a quarter for a few seconds, we would all run out of money in a minute or two, so best to stop. We walked out into the rain, wet from the weather, not the experience, and headed back to our team hotel. To this day, we haven't spoken about it past that week. It's like we all want to forget the confusing sexual nature of the entire thing.

GOLDEN CORRAL

One night, immediately following a tough road win in the D-League, our coach walked into the locker room and said "that game was like fucking your sister. It was good, but not as good as it should have been."

Then we all went to Golden Corral.

48 HOURS

In January 2015, immediately after being cut from my Taiwanese team, I got on a flight from Taipei to Manila with intent to sign with a Philippines team called Talk N Text. I built a pretty good reputation in Korea as one of the best players in Asia so I came in with a decent amount of Philippine media hype, which felt unusual for a mid-season signing.

The team picked me up from the airport and immediately took me to a gigantic luxury mall, fed me a fantastic meal, and told me all the plans the team had for me. We took photos and did interviews for the media. It was great.

As the welcome wagon was coming to its end, the team GM made sure to let me know there would be one potential concern with my sticking on the team. He informed me that they have height restrictions in the Philippines and only two teams are allowed to have a player over the height of 6' 9". To be honest, a lot of countries have weird rules around height so it wasn't that crazy to hear, but I was a little shook because I'm 6'10" on the number. I'm not 6'9" or 6'8-½". I'm as 6'10" as 6'10" gets.

"But you're really 6'9" right?" The GM seemed confident in this process. "Everyone lies, so that's a start. But if you are *slightly* over, we can help with that."

I shrugged and said ok. I figured it didn't really matter anyway. Stretching is the hard part. Slouching is easy. It felt moot from that perspective.

The GM was confident until the next morning when the team measured me. On their wall I actually measured at 6'10-¼" and I could see the sweat accrue on his forehead as he tried to figure it out. It was decided that I'd still practice but that I would do extra exercises that had been 'proven' to shrink someone slightly by tightening the right muscles.

So after a tough practice in 100% humidity and 97 degree weather, they put me in the weight room to execute a series of leg and back exercises that, if done properly, would shrink my body. They were designed to leave me dehydrated as well, so I couldn't drink water while doing them. And all of that ignores the fact that I'd likely also be bad at basketball for at least a week with random sore spots that I wasn't used to. Still, I did it all. A $20,000 paycheck was waiting for me on the other end of this ridiculous practice, so the choice was clear.

I must reiterate that I did think this was all a moot point. Here I was giving myself a massive headache and breaking down my body to achieve something that baggy sweats and a slight knee bend could achieve. I truly thought this was all over the top for what the goal was, but I trusted the process.

The following day, as the manager and GM were driving me to get my official measurement, they explained the process in full. The first thing I needed to be aware of was that other teams could be there to witness the measurement as a formality. This was rare, they explained, but if another team felt there was something nefarious about the measuring process, they could call for a second measurement on site.

I was assured that other teams nearly never attend these procedures because of how mundane they are and, on the off-chance they did challenge the results, I'd just get measured again and that'll be the end of it. Seemed easy enough.

When we arrived, every team in the league had sent two proxies to watch my measurement ceremony. As I mentioned before, the Korean hype around my name made a lot of other teams worried that I might disrupt the power balance in the Philippine league so they were incredibly incentivized to make sure that I wasn't over the limit.

I was sitting there waiting thinking this was insane. I could also barely stand up. I hadn't had liquid in 16 hours and my body was sore in new and different ways. I picture myself looking like Tyrone Biggums dressed as Dennis Rodman for Halloween. But, again, all I had to do was slouch, so no big deal.

It was now time to find out why slouching was never going to work. I was not measured standing up against a wall like every other time I'd been measured in my life. I walked into the measuring room, and there were numbers written on a table.

OH. FUCK.

I was going to be laying down for this process, which I did not anticipate in the slightest. When I laid down on what looked like some sort of human sized butcher's table, someone came and held my hips down. Someone else ran rulers underneath my back to make sure I was laying as flat as possible. I had to tell them I got a little scoliosis and a lot of ass because they kept thinking I was cheating the system. I wasn't.

It was truly wild because as all of this was happening, I was actively trying my best to be smaller. It was excruciating because, by design, the process took minutes and my muscles were all fatigued. I couldn't just suddenly shrink, I had to appear like I was always smaller. So I had to hold that shit tight for a long ass time.

I must have held my breath and clinched my legs muscles with all I had for a full two or three minutes before they let me go. Biggest exhale of my life, weed notwithstanding. They announced my measured height. It was exactly 6'9". I did my little Tiger fist pump, finger gunned the coach like Shooter McGavin, and was making my way out when one of the attending witnesses objected to my measurement.

Immediately, one of the officials grabbed me and stopped me from walking out and they laid me right back down for the exact same three minute process. Whatever I had been able to hold in before, I no longer had the ability to find a second time. I was drenched in sweat, but fully dehydrated, tired and red eyed, with a bunch of rulers running up and down my back while 20 unfamiliar Filipino faces stared down at numbers that I could not see.

When the time was up the second time, the number was said aloud. 6'9-⅛ ". Some of the strangers audibly cheered at the news and made their way out. I sat there exhausted, unsure of what would come next.

I assumed I'd get another shot at it in the morning or something, but instead I was handed an already printed out return to USA plane ticket and was driven to the airport. I hadn't even realized they had grabbed my stuff from the hotel. And just like that, 48 hours in Manila were over.

OH 2

Maybe a decade after I left, I ran into a girl I slightly remembered from college. Maybe we hung out once? With a group? My memory was weak. She helped fill in the gaps.

"Rod Benson! OMG! The biggest prude at Cal! Ha!"

"I'm sorry. What? A prude? All I wanted was a girlfriend the entire time!"

"No you didn't. Everyone knew. 'Rod Benson is gonna take you to his room and show you all his posters and his computer and not make a move.'"

WHO IS EVERYONE?

THE LAST DAY

On my last day ever in Korea, I packed my shit up nicely, leaving a pile of sweats and jackets behind. Every year I'd come with two full bags of clothes at the start, and during the course of the season I'd accrue two full bags of new clothes from the team. I never had much choice but to start leaving a lot of it behind. I only needed so much HUMMEL brand gear.

I never knew where all that shit went after I left. I assumed they just threw it all away because no one else in the whole country could fit my clothes. They even had US ladies sizing for everything. It's one thing trying to give away XL sweats. It's another trying to give away sweats that are the same size but the label reads 9XL. Wherever they went, they were never there the next season.

But there was no longer a next season. There was just the end. What a weird feeling.

I walked into the kitchen to get some rice and steak (the same meal the Ajumas made me for years). As soon as I walked in, my teammate Yun Ho Young walked up to me. He was crying. He doesn't speak even one word of English, so we never had one real conversation, but we were brothers. We're the same age, which is a big deal in Korea. We played through some wild shit. We even had an entire arc together as two thirds of the 'triple tower.' I cried, too. It was unexpected as hell.

I guess I should have expected that people would be sad I was leaving, but by the end of my career I had become jaded. Guys were signed and cut so frequently and mercilessly that I started to assume no one cared about any of this. How could we, in perpetuity?

I remember when I was cut from the Nets thinking about how often and routine it was for guys like Kidd and VC to meet a dude for a couple weeks and then never see them again. It was in their best interest not to care, lest they get upset every time a friend leaves.

Eventually, I became the same way. There were just so many D-League camps, mini camps, training camps, new countries, etc. I must have played with 1000 guys, and I can probably name 50 off the top of my head right now.

So yea, when Yun Ho Young started crying, I began to contextualize myself a bit more. I wasn't there for ten days. I was there for eight years. That wasn't nothing.

I felt more arms. The Ajumas stopped preparing food and they were crying, too. If Yun Ho Young had been my brother, these had been my grandmothers. And still, it was unexpected.

I collected my food, teary eyed, and said my last goodbyes, knowing I would likely never see any of them again.

I still haven't.

THE FIRST DAY

I don't know for sure which is my earliest basketball memory, but I know that it could be the time I walked into the Boys and Girls Club of Lakeside, CA and immediately kicked a basketball laying on the ground. A counselor picked up the ball, walked over to me and said "a basketball is not for kicking."

I felt embarrassed and began to look at what other kids were doing with the ball. Emulating them, I began to try to shoot around until it became fun. I left that day with interest in joining the 5 and 6 year old division of the house basketball league.

I spent that time learning to love basketball. I met my mentor, Russell, at the Club and he taught me a great deal in a short time. He was disabled, and I think the fact that he was in a wheelchair made him less threatening to parents. Because of that, we did everything together. He introduced me to Magic Johnson and UCLA. He showed me the Star Wars films and made sure I understood we were seeing episode 4, 5, and 6. He introduced me to email. He taught me how to log into a network on my Commodore 64 and send messages. In 1990, he may as well have taught me magic. I even helped him assemble and disassemble his chair and load it into his Ford Escort, a high amount of growth for a 5 year old.

But nothing was more special than basketball. He knew far more about the game than whoever else worked at the Boys and Girls Club and he took interest in helping me to learn. If the camcorder videos are to be believed, I was a dominant rebounder right from the start, and he helped me run with that. It was the first time I felt community in my life and I began to really care about the game and that team.

We had made it to the six and under championship a couple of months later and nothing had ever felt more important or exciting. What's more was that my dad; who I almost never saw nor had communication with, was supposed to come into town that day. What perfect timing that scheduled custody time coincided with my first great achievement! It was like everything was coming together in the most perfect way.

I sat and waited for him to pick me up for the game, knowing Russell and the team were waiting for me, watching as valuable warm-up minutes ticked away.

He finally showed up very late, but with just enough time to take me to the Boys and Girls Club and win my first trophy. Instead, he got on the 8 freeway and drove the other direction.

I distinctly remember looking back through the rear window of the car as the city of Lakeside vanished in the distance, hoping he might change his mind and turn around. He didn't. I spent the entire ride to Los Angeles crying in protest. I didn't really enjoy basketball or him the same after that.

ID FOR LUDA

We used to wake up way too early for school. I think my mom really just tried to give my brother a lot of runway. It didn't matter if school was at 6am or Noon, my brother was going to wake up just in time to take his sweet ass time. That's what made this day so weird, my mom didn't just let the alarms go off at 5:30, she woke us up.

"There was some big plane crash in New York. Turn on the news."

I turned on the news just in time to see the second plane fly into the towers, a moment nobody watching live expected. When it hit, I was desensitized because I thought it was a replay of the first. If I turn on a baseball or hockey game and someone immediately hits a home run or scores a goal, I assume I'm seeing a replay. It's always a shock to learn it was live. It was the same feeling this time. The realization that I just watched all these people expire was crazy.

We still went to school, like everyone did. We didn't know what else to do. When I got to AP Statistics, Dr Stuckenshnider already had the TV cart rolled into the front of the room. He was crying. Everyone was crying. I wasn't, if only because the gravity didn't hit me. These were wealthy kids who had families and friends on both coasts. I didn't. I sat there and watched in horror, the same way I would watch a movie about the same thing.

Four months later and I'd just been named the 'hottest recruit on the west coast.' This was in large part because I was a very late bloomer and there were slim pickens left in the talent pool, but still.

When it was time to take my official visits, my mom put her foot down again.

"He's not getting on a commercial plane," she announced to both the coaches of Oregon and Cal, respectively, "not after 9/11. So figure that out."

I personally wasn't too concerned about the fact that the 9/11 terrorists used planes, I was just scared of planes in general. My mother, however, had been permanently shook by those planes running into the twin towers. She was the lynchpin in my recruiting, so the coaches knew if they wanted me they had to get creative and appease her.

At first, she was going to make them drive me to the locations, but all of us told her that was not at all an option. I didn't feel like I had a ton of agency, but I definitely told her I wasn't driving to Oregon when there was a plane. She capitulated and told the coaches they could fly me, they just had to fly me out of the Carlsbad Airport. If you haven't heard of the Carlsbad Airport, that's her point.

To pull this off, Cal and Oregon coordinated. I'd fly from Carlsbad to Eugene, from Eugene to San Francisco, and from Oakland to Carlsbad again. These dudes really did a ride share to get me to their schools. I was not good enough at basketball to warrant any of these demands, but again, they did it.

When I got to Oregon, it was sunny as hell. I only remember that because every single person I met told me it was. Every single person. I swear there would just be someone walking across the street and out of nowhere they would yell "wow what great weather for this time of year, right?!"

It's hard to remember all the details of the trip, but I do recall that the Lukes took me out and showed me around. Those were some white boy rockstars, for sure. Still nobody talked about them. They only mentioned the sun.

We toured the old gym, which creaked with every step. They definitely needed to stop playing games there, even if it was awesome. And I remember my jersey sitting in the locker room with #0 on it. That was my first time seeing my name on a Jersey. God, I wanted to take it with me when I left.

"That's a violation." – The NCAA

I landed at SFO and it was raining. I remember because it's all everyone would talk about. It's like everyone was hellbent on alerting me that I had just missed the good weather. This I should have actually paid attention to, because it rained the first two months of my freshman year at Cal. It was an omen.

My trip to Cal was certainly more interesting. The first thing they did was take me to EA Sports and promise me a job there. I accepted. This was all a ruse because Redwood City is nowhere near Berkeley, but in a new city I couldn't tell shit for directions, so it was what it was.

When I met the guys on the team, they could certainly tell I was different. If not by how I spoke or how corny I was, definitely by my AOL screen name.

"It's Ludacrispychickn," I replied when prompted.

"Luda what? Your name is Ludacrispychicken?" Burl Toler couldn't believe it.

None of the folks in the room, composed of young football and basketball players, could believe it.

"So who got a ID for Luda?" someone asked the room. It was already hella funny.

"I got one," Bryce Copeland said. I don't really even know Bryce Copeland to this day, but I've had his ID for years so I'll remember the name forever.

Then they took me to some party that was kinda boring, but I could feel the camaraderie among them. I enjoyed that.

When I got back to Carlsbad, I told my mom I wanted to go to Cal. When she asked why, I gave a laundry list of reasons. Those were mostly lies. The actual reason was they had Jordans and it was a good school. It was that simple. Some kids aren't that complicated, even the complicated ones.

I guess I could have saved them all the trouble, but it really wasn't on me. It was on Osama Bin Laden.

PANIC ATTACK

It was my Junior year at Cal and we had just beaten Oregon in Eugene. I don't remember the game details but I dunked on some folks, got some impressive buckets, etc. I was used to playing well against the mid teams cause they didn't really try to scheme me. That's not a good thing. I just think I wasn't consistent enough yet for other teams to make me their focus.

After the game, riding a wave of positive emotions and armed with a very good knowledge of the city of Eugene, I went out to Taylor's, Eugene's most problematic venue. I'd been there many times before with the homie Sam and his crew of South Eugene HS kids.

He wasn't there that night, though. It was me and my teammate who also balled out that night and we were on a mission. I knew exactly what I was doing, showing up all 6'10" at this bar right after a game. The attention was swift and aggressive. Within minutes, he and I had a chorus of female Ducks looking to enter the Flying V.

This was actually not normal for me. Berkeley didn't have fans that cared enough to act weird around us (or me specifically), and we didn't go out on the road after games we won very often, cause it didn't happen very often. Plus, we may not have known what to do in the road city or the city might be dead, even if we did win. Annnd even if all of that happened, we might have to travel right away so there wouldn't be time. This was hands down a 1/1 opportunity. So, yea, we let it happen.

I had settled into a conversation with a woman that was actually pretty cool. I don't remember the topic, but it was deep and meaningful. It was political and ambitious. It was interrupted when two absolute dimes walked in. I didn't even notice them but the woman I was talking to did.

"Eww. Fuck those bitches," she said. She clearly knew them.

I looked up.

Well damn.

"Why?"

"Because they're fucking whores who just fuck basketball players. So gross."

"Would you excuse me for a minute?"

In a move I had never done before and have not done since, I literally walked right up to the two dimes and introduced myself. We were walking out of the bar five minutes later. The first woman's conversation was deep, but theirs went deeper.

I woke up so hungover. My teammate was shaking the shit out of me. My eyes were trying to focus as he was yelling at me.

"Rod! We gotta go! Now!"

I started putting on clothes with my mouth open. The dime I ended up with was laying there. Or something. I think. We were somewhere dark and the light was barely creeping in.

I don't even know how we got back to the hotel, but we did. Luckily the hotel we stayed at in Eugene was funky and had like nineteen points of entry, because coaches did always watch the halls. I went into my room, changed into the team sweats and went down to the bus.

I'm about to tell you something I truly did not understand until now. I really really thought I pulled it off and tricked everyone into thinking I was sober the whole day. We had practice in Corvallis and I played decently. I smiled at people and said hi and shit. I hadn't been late to anything and I asked questions in the film session. I was attentive the whole day. I went to bed thinking I clowned everyone.

In actuality I bet I smelled like vodka and ass from a mile away, I sleep-walked through practice, and the coaches had a panic attack until I dropped 20 the next night.

CUT 6

"You did better than I expected you would, considering how old you are."

Jeff Van Gundy had a way with words.

The next day I was flying back from Houston to LA. I was off Team USA.

BESTIES

In my second to last season in Korea, I played for Wonju DB. Wonju is the name of the city and DB, which is short for Dongbu, is the name of the corporation that runs the team.

This was my second stint on this team after spending a few years on Ulsan Hyundai Mobis. So every time we played against Mobis, it was a big deal for me because my time on Hyundai didn't go well. I didn't like them and they didn't like me.

In that season, Mobis went small with their Americans which was unusual for Korea because most teams bring in the biggest guys they can find (and why they eventually established height limits). Because of this, every time we played them I would have a monster game stats-wise. I'd go for 30 and 20 and look directly at their bench to let them know they played themselves.

Despite the fact that I had big numbers, we were not always winning these games. That's because they were a well coached, talented team led by their American guard, Nate Miller. He was a bowling ball of a guard who could do a lot of things well. He couldn't really guard me, but he didn't need to. They had a scheme and a game plan that worked for them. But when he did match up with me, I think he took exception to all my trash talking. Why wouldn't he? Without knowing all the history, he assumed I was talking to him and he would get angry. This man could really mix it up when we both got angry.

One day I saw him out in a bar in Seoul and I was pretty lit. I don't really remember what I said to him but I felt like I was trying to build a relationship and I wanted him to know that it wasn't about him. I disliked his team, but I also knew what it was like to be a part of that nightmare. I just wanted him to know that I understood, you know?

We played them a few weeks later and I felt like I had a new friend. In between plays I kept making comments to him and laughing and this and that. Finally, we were lined up for a free throw and I made a joke about something or other.

He looked me straight in the eye and yelled "Bro I don't know you!!"

So yea. We were not friends.

Note: when researching for this story I found out that he passed in June 2022. I wish I had gotten to know him now.

FROM BREEZE TO POKE

Winter 2005 to Spring 2006 was a very busy time. It was the end of my collegiate career. There was graduation. There was an injury and there was a homeless person driving my mom's van around town. There was a lot. My own problems be damned, I was constantly in other people's business. There was always so much drama that it was easy.

"This person did this thing, can you believe it?"

Yes.

The tea as the New Year approached was that I had two sophomore teammates who were dating the absolute worst women. I can't say that these women were that bad with more perspective, but I can say that for the time and situation, one that involved a lot of drama, these ladies took the cake. Jen was a swimmer and Claudia was on the Water Polo team, both notoriously horny sports. They were each their own menace.

Why this mattered to me was because these teammates lived in the same building as I did, in the unit directly below. So in my apartment it was Richard, JGant, and myself and in the apartment below, it was Will (aka Willy Davis), Terrance Hunt (Thunt), and Stimson (Stims). All six of us were in a relationship at the same time, so the house should have been tame, but it was not because Jen and Claudia were really out here.

Both of these women had a very public sexual history. I'm not going to sit here on my high horse and act like the basketball team were some saints, because they weren't. But Hunt and Willy were actually just good, regular guys with a full emotional range, and none of the same ego as the rest of us. White guys who didn't play a lot were often cool like that. This was them. So when Jen and Claudia showed up, us older guys felt protective. These women were going to eat my teammates alive.

We stopped liking Jen because when she and THunt first got together, he was the last guy of three that day. Yes, the first time they ever had sex, he was the third person for her that day. We know this because she literally told everyone every detail. She made a bet to sleep with three dudes, and THunt was last. She won the bet. He even found out and he acted like she was nothing to him.

"Her name is in my phone as 'Breeze.' I don't care," he said as he took his tenth shower of the day.

Claudia was different. She didn't do the same amount of dirt, but she did things right in front of Davis that she could then somehow spin into whatever story she wanted. For example, there was an entire semester where a Golden State Warrior was kicking it with her on campus, often with Willy Davis in the room.

"You know they're fucking, right?"

"No. Actually," Willy is very intelligent, "while they do have a budding friendship, she's helping him wi–"

"No man. They're fucking. Why the hell is this NBA dude always with your girlfriend? Really think about it," I would plead.

"I appreciate your opinion, Rod. I'll give it some consideration."

Both he and Hunt were too far gone to see what was happening. While this bothered me, it used to get Stims up in arms. For starters, Stims has an even bigger personality than I do. That dude will verbally or physically make his presence known in any room within seconds. Yes, even more than me. He also holds onto things. He's reading this right now plotting when he can tell the story of how the bacon grease from the Foreman Grill got on him.

"Do I have to give Claudia the Kielbasa just to show you who she is, Willy?" Stims was less kind, but also always funny.

He also refers to his dick as THE Kielbasa.

"I hear you, Stims. Yea, I think I'm going to end it," Davis would always say, but never do.

Since Stims was an asshole and I was fast becoming one, we decided to take matters into our own hands. If these boys couldn't save themselves, we would have to do it for them.

The first plan was to take out Claudia, who was still definitely fucking some Warriors, and had added a Cal football player as well. We were able to confirm the football player because they went into a room at a frat house and smashed, then she went directly to Willy's and stayed the night. We saw the whole thing and told him, he hit us with:

"Really? That's hurtful. I'm definitely going to end it."

He didn't.

We figured we needed hard evidence to convince him, but we needed to know how she kept spinning the truth. What was she saying to him that kept him from ending it? We had to get answers, so we set up a trap.

While Willy and Claudia were out, Stims and I went into Willy's room and placed Stims's RAZR phone in a Christmas stocking Willy had hanging above his bed. The RAZR, we hoped, was a slim enough profile that it would go undetected while we listened to their conversation via a phone call to my phone.

We dialed my number, planted the phone, and went into Stims' room to listen. We heard them come back into the room and start talking. It was ass because we really couldn't hear shit, save for rustling. All of a sudden we could hear everything:

"Do you hear breathing?"

"Yes, actually."

"What the fuck is this?"

"Yea what is that?!"

There was a knock on Stims's door a second later. We opened the door and Claudia and Davis were there holding Stims's phone. Busted.

That was our last attempt at trying to get rid of Claudia. Their senses were heightened and they just started keeping the details secret enough that we stopped. I do think that level of seriousness Stims and I both had made Willy really reconsider, and Claudia didn't want the stress of us harassing her. They broke up a long while later, so I guess in the end, it worked? It took years to find out.

As for Jen, that was an entirely different set of events. Hunt was a lot better at making it seem like he didn't care. He'd move on, hook up with someone else, declare that it was over, then Stims would shoot me a late night text like

> you won't believe who's here

There was a solid month where we thought it was over, but he kept texting and smiling one day. When he went to take his fourth shower that day, we grabbed his phone. Passcodes weren't a thing. He kept texting with someone named 'Poke.' We pulled the number and sure enough it was Jen. He had just changed her name from Breeze to Poke.

I'm unsure if what followed was planned to help THunt or if it was regular shitty college behavior but it was wild. One day, one of Stims's football homies, Bo, was over and Jen came by early to meet with THunt, but THunt wasn't home from practice yet.

This is hard to explain, but their apartment layout matters for this one. There were two windows facing the front of the apartment, one belonging to Stims's bedroom and the other was for the kitchen. The other two bedrooms were back past the living area. So to get to one of the other two bedrooms, you'd have to pass Stims's room and the kitchen.

That said, Jen took a liking to Bo. Bo and Jen went into Stims's room and smashed. As they were doing it, THunt came home and could hear it, but just assumed it was Stim and his girlfriend.

When they were finished, both Bo and Jen jumped out of Stim's window, to the front of the apartment. Bo went home and Jen walked back into the apartment through the front door, went into THunt's room and closed the door.

It was when we laid out all these events in plain English for THunt and he still kept seeing her that we knew this was all a fool's errand. Maybe it was our collective senior vanity project. Maybe it was just mean and we were bored. Whatever the reasons, I learned that you can't stop someone from loving someone else, even if it's killing them. I never really tried again.

ADVICE 2

After college, a few weeks into my pro training, I asked an NBA veteran what advice he had for me as a rookie.

"It's cheaper to keep her," he replied.

Then we ate hot dogs. It was *his* BBQ, after all.

THE RED EYE

At UC Berkeley they have a program for incoming students to get a head start called Summer Bridge. The athletics program uses Summer Bridge to get freshman athletes in early so they can acclimate and get credits before school officially begins in the fall.

For me, Summer Bridge started on July 5, 2002. I know this because on July 4th, my mom, brother, and myself piled into our minivan and drove from San Diego to the Bay Area to stay with family ahead of my first day as a collegiate athlete.

I had never before met these family members, so it was wild how excited they were to know I would be starting at Cal coon. They were having a BBQ in Richmond to celebrate and had bought fireworks for the occasion. I grabbed a roman candle and was casually shooting colorful explosions into the distance when the end of the stick itself blew up right in front of my face. The flash was bright and my ears began to ring immediately. When I came to and got to take a look at myself in a mirror, my right eye was completely bloodshot.

The next day was my first day of college and I looked like I had pink-eye. Literally the first thing I had to do was go to get my school ID. I probably would have waited had I known that I would look like I had pinkeye on my ID for the next four years.

The second thing I did was move into what would be my future dorm. I was actually super excited because I knew who my other freshman teammates were but I had never actually seen them play. This is a foreign concept now, but back then rankings would just come out and I'd be like "who the hell is Matt Haryasz and why is he ranked one slot higher than me?" For many of us, those questions were answered in college. Since I had no idea what my teammates were supposed to look like, I was just going up to random people asking if they were Richard Midgley or David Paris. Lucky for me it wouldn't be long before I would meet both of them at once.

The last thing on the agenda for my first day was study hall. Keep in mind that we had not had a class yet so there wasn't really anything to study, so it was more of a light seminar teaching us how to use and find other academic resources. This study hall was exclusively for incoming athletes so there must have been three hundred people there, all meeting for the first time, all sure that this sham study hall was meaningless.

Even if we had already had classes, which we hadn't, this was the first time that the volleyball girls, the soccer girls, the baseball dudes and the water polo guys were all meeting for the first time. There was no way they were going to sit and study quietly for two hours. When I walked in, the space was already hella rowdy because a bunch of teenagers were looking for potential sexual matches.

I took my seat at the basketball table and finally met Richard and David. Before I could even introduce myself, Richard looked me dead in the eye and tilted his head.

"What's wrong with your fuckin' eye?" he asked without hesitation or restraint.

I, being the long-winded person I am, proceeded to tell Richard the entire story in good faith. He listened with intent, nodding, and asking questions. As I wrapped up the story, Richard asked another question.

"So your eye is just red now?"

"Yea," I started, "for now. But I'd appreciate it if you didn't talk about it. I have sensitive eyes."

"What's that mean?"

"It means the more I think about them or talk about them, the more they start to get irritated and watery and it looks like I'm crying."

"Oh ok mate. No problem."

I leaned back into my books, again, studying nothing because I hadn't had class yet. Everyone was going wild in this study hall, so it was hard to concentrate, but I was determined to leave this session ahead of the game.

Out of nowhere, Richard stuck his finger right in front of my red eye, inches in front of my face, and left it there.

Ha. That's actually funny. Just wait it out.

30 seconds later it was still there. A minute later it was still there. My eyes began to get crazy watery.

I had dealt with enough bullies to know that the first rule of bullies is to ignore them. Everyone eventually runs out of steam. Everyone, that is, except Richard Midgley. To that point, I had never seen anyone with the willpower, resolve, and straight up desire to be *that much* of an asshole.

It was shocking how locked in he was, finger extended in front of my face, for what must have been three, four, five minutes. The man truly was born without fucks to give. David, who I haven't mentioned yet, was just loving this whole song and dance. He always had this way of laughing along but making it seem like he was innocent.

"Shit don't look at me! Richard trippin!"

There was a point where I went from surviving to despair. I was truly shook that my own teammate would take my words and use them against me for laughs right away.

What a Judas ass bitch.

It felt like the room kept getting louder, the finger was still sitting there, I could barely see the book in front of me that no one had assigned me to read, and my eyes kept getting more watery. Finally I stood up and slammed my book down. It all happened so fast, I didn't consider that when a nearly 7 foot kid slams his book, the room gets quiet.

So when I then screamed "YOU JUST DON'T GIVE A FUCK ABOUT MY FUTURE," everyone heard it. Everyone.

I looked like I was crying because eye water was streaming down my face. I finally understood what I must have looked like when I scanned the room and everyone looked at me as if they were attempting to determine if I was on a 'special' scholarship.

Embarrassed as all hell, I grabbed my stuff and walked out and back to the dorm. I went to bed that night thinking that college might be much more ruthless even than I thought. But, shit, my future was still in tact. That was all that mattered.

EMAILS FROM BILL 6

From: BILL

To: ???@eurobasket.com

Sent: 9/30/2009 8:41:55 A.M. Eastern Daylight Time

Subj: Re: Rod Benson

---: I will check with other agent and see if he is offering him. My guess he is not. So, you can offer him. We just need to know by Monday because that is when he leaves for China. Again, please let me know the team to protect you, and of course, I must check them out. You can wait until I speak with the Greek agent before telling me the team. I have placed a call to him. Thank you for your interest in Rod.

Bill

. . .

In a message dated 9/30/2009 8:34:45 A.M. Eastern
Daylight Time, ???@eurobasket.com writes:

Bill,

Thank you for the email. Firstly because i know
and as you said you had

players in Greece, i dont want any conflicts and
give offer for Rod when

you have also other Greek agent talking and
pushing Rod in the Greek

market. I like Rod, i've seen him in 2007 when he
finished first rebounder

in NBDL that season and i can say that he has the
skills to play here but i

want to tell me if you gave Rod also to other
Greek agent.

The situation i talked to Rod is very good, the
salary will be 15k per

month, money paid on time. They will make the
final decision inside the

weekend or Monday. So if the things move good for
Rod he must be ready to

come sometime close to the end of next week.

Regards,

URL : http://www.eurobasket.com/about.asp

Author & Scouter

URL : http://www.eurobasket.com/gre/gre.asp

URL : http://www.nbadraft.net/articles.asp

WE NEED A MINUTE

It was spring 2008 and I was playing on the Dakota Wizards. We were on the road in Albuquerque, New Mexico, which was always ass. The city itself wasn't so bad, especially considering most everything was *better* than Bismarck. It was the arena the team played the games in. It was by far the worst in the league.

The Thunderbirds played in an old rodeo hall (is that a thing?) that was definitely not built with basketball in mind. It was on some fairgrounds that were old and literally dusty. The locker rooms were all weird and had horrible sight lines, the basketball surface was placed on top of a dirt pit and it was cold as hell.

Beyond that, no one attended these games. There would be 30 fans at a game simply because the townspeople felt they had something better to do – in Albuquerque. Every time we played there, it felt like a gimmick.

One game, my man Carlos Powell was going off. He probably finished with 40. Hardly anyone saw the performance, though, save for a few people, because 70 people attended the game and it wasn't televised. One of those people was a 12 year old kid who was seated right under the basket. Every time Carlos Powell scored, the kid cheered very loudly for Kasib Powell.

"That's it Kasib Powell! Keep killing it!"

It was kind of funny, because the kid was clearly confused and mixing up Carlos and Kasib. The entire rodeo hall was lightly laughing along with this innocent child cheering for the wrong Powell. I think Carlos was fine with it, though. The arena was so damn quiet that even one person cheering made it more lively. Carlos ate it up.

"Kasib! You the man!" the kid continued with each of Los' buckets.

"Kasssiiiibbbbbb! For twooooo!!!"

Carlos started to smile. I would have, too. He was unstoppable and this kid was hyping him and him alone.

Finally, after one of these exchanges, Carlos was running back on defense and he yelled to the kid "My name's Carlos Powell by the way."

The crowd chuckled collectively. Carlos finally said what we were all thinking. The kid shot RIGHT back:

"Yea I know. I just like Kasib more."

HE DELIVERED THIS WITH A STRAIGHT FACE.

Look.

Carlos is a pretty tough dude. I've never really seen him rattled or anything close. But on this day I watched a child snatch his soul. All 70 people in the arena started laughing so damn hard. I feel like the refs called the first ever 'ayo we need a minute' timeout in basketball history. Our team was laughing. The other team was laughing. The kid, realizing he pulled off one of the great long-con jokes of our time, started waving his arms to hype up the laughter as if he was giving an encore at The Apollo.

It was, by far, the most hilarious moment in the history of my career. That kid gotta be like 28 by now. Let's find him and watch his tight five cause he definitely has one.

FANS.

Do you rep your city? Do you go hard for Detroit? New York?

Even if you don't rep your city, do you rep a guy? Did he get traded?

No one needs to tell you who to root for because you're not casual. You read blogs and watch video breakdowns. You're better at Twitter. Admit it.

You're not the crazy guy who breaks his TV because the Broncos got a first down, right? Of course not. You understand the sport differently. Your dad put you in a jersey the day you were born. You definitely believe in free will.

DD
DIFFERENT
DUDE™

HANDS DOWN REAL QUICK

The very first thing I was interested in when I got to Korea was finding a tailor. Not only was I now flush with sweet cash, but I had gotten some shirts done when I was in Beijing a year prior that were quite nice. I use 'quite nice' on purpose because I had never worn anything that actually fit my body before those shirts. The first time I put one on, I looked in the mirror and said "oh that's quite nice."

After a year or two of working with basic tailors who essentially made suits and shirts, I thought I'd maximized that potential in Korea.

Some time later, I was out at the clurb and ran into the very stylish Sandrin brothers. The Sandrin Bros (or Lee Bros if it pleases you) are half Korean brothers who played in the Korean league with me and who speak the language. They also wore clothes that had to be custom, because they were well fitted despite their 6'8" frames. They knew things I didn't. Specifically, they knew a tailor who had imagination.

I asked them how they get the spicy shit and they gave me the contact of a man who goes by the name 'Mr Tony.'

"He can make anything."

"Anything?!"

"Anything."

I called Mr Tony the next week and he was very excitable on the phone. He spoke pretty good English for having a thick accent, but he talked like he learned English from a mob boss or something.

Say the words 'why I outta' out loud. Now imagine Al Capone saying that with a Korean accent. If he was the guy who could make different shit, he certainly came off as a dude who does exactly that.

The next day I got into a taxi and headed south from Yongin to Osan, where the air force base is located. It's only a 40 minute ride, but the starting and ending locations could not be more different. The areas around the bases in Korea are basically mini America towns and this one might have been the most American of them all. The army base had full American brands and chains on it, and even used USD. If the base was real America, the rest of Osan felt like a weird mist mash of old Korean and American war culture.

I walked in and Tony already knew who I was from TV.

"Benson! You good boy. Man you can get the rebounds and the triple tower oh my God! Aye you like Crown royal? Of course you Benson Strong man! Fighting!"

Everyone used to reference the 'triple tower' because that was the nickname of myself and two of my teammates known for our defensive prowess, and everyone there says 'fighting' as if it means 'Let's go!'

We sat there, got drunk, and concocted damn near a whole wardrobe that was fire as hell. I spent some cash, but that cash was well worth it. I now had an entire closet of unique and imaginative clothes that actually fit my body. What a treat.

When I got back to LA, I was styling, bro. Styling!

Every single thing I wore, people would be like "where… the fuck… did you buy that?"

"Got a guy in Korea, player."

One of those people was my homie Mitch. Mitch and I had been friends for years. He had a big personality, a bigger penchant for turning up, and an even bigger penchant for drinking too much. We worked well as friends back then because I was similar. I found the one person alive who not only could keep up with me, but also wanted to.

He wanted to come to Korea and get his own clothes made, so in 2018 we finally made that happen. Mitch flew out to Incheon airport and we went almost directly to Mr Tony who was awaiting us.

Before this moment, I had never brought anyone to Mr Tony besides my brother, and I had never given Mr Tony so much lead time about my potential arrival. This was different now because Mitch booked a month in advance. Mr Tony could hardly contain his excitement.

"You need to stay night in Osan. I know a good hotel. I'm chamber of commerce they have to fuck with me for the good rate! Then we can get fucked up really good."

The man was so pumped that I figured I could give him the chance to show me the real Osan. It would be fun to do something different. I booked a hotel in the center of town and Mitch and I went out there.

When Mitch and I arrived in Osan, Mr Tony had two full handles of Crown Royal waiting for us. Three total people. I could feel that his ambition for the night maybe exceeded mine, but I liked the chaotic energy of it all. Mitch loved it even more. He and Mr Tony hit it off immediately, and both may have been drunk-drunk 30 minutes in.

After we wrapped the design portion of the evening, Tony said he had a whole plan for the night so we followed him. We went to some lamb spot (I feel like in Korea you just say the type of food followed by the word spot always), and they kept getting drunker. It's a little unfair to say it like that because so was I, but they were on something extra. It wasn't even the liquor, it was the possibilities!

After dinner, Mr Tony said the next spot was the norebang. Norebang, which I believe directly translates to 'music room,' essentially is private karaoke. You've likely done it before and just called it karaoke. It's not weird at all unless you go with a Korean person. Going with a Korean to a norebang is a totally different experience than going alone or with Americans.

Normally, when I go to the norebang without Koreans, there's an older lady working the desk. She signals how many people, I signal back the number and she nods. Then she calmly walks us to an empty room setup for singing, motions to soju, I say yes, and we get right to some Teenage Dirtbag. Whenever we are done, we are done.

When I went with Mr Tony and Mitch, none of the beats were the same. First, he asked if we wanted to go to a 'good' or 'regular' norebang. I had been asked this many times and always answered with "I don't care."

Good or bad norebangs, by other folks' definition, always felt the same to me.

"Whatever, my guy," I said, giving him control.

So, no, I wasn't trippin when we walked in and he started directing the older lady at the front desk. She and Mr Tony spoke for a while, then he gestured for us to follow him. We sat in the room, which wasn't the fanciest (my bad) and we started doing our thang.

I say 'started,' because before I could open the book of songs, the front desk woman was back with a few other older women wearing dresses short enough to be offensive to even the most hardened sensibilities.

"Which one?" Mr Tony asked Mitch and me.

I didn't know what was happening, but since then I learned that essentially Koreans double these places as low grade brothels. These women were ours to choose from for the night.

Everyone trained their eyes on me because I was the 'celebrity' in the room. I wouldn't even call it staring. It was like a wanting look: one that signaled my approval of the whole ordeal. I was the talent.

I could stop this whole train but I didn't. I really wanted to see what came next, but I also had no interest. I was in a relationship, not cheating, and generally didn't even consider prostitution as a thing. And, if all of that was not true, I still definitely had no desire to grab a 55 year old Korean prostitute. It was a lot to consider in three seconds.

"I'm cool yall," I said in a way I hope didn't offend.

Mr Tony wasn't having it.

"Come on Benson! You don't like girls? Hey you said you wanted a bad place!"

It was then I realized that folks had always been rating norebangs by the quality of the prostitutes. Six years of understanding happened in one statement.

Mitch was clearly more conflicted. He was looking at me for guidance. Surely I could offer him some solace? I could not. I basically just nodded and told him to do whatever makes him happy. He took this as a green light as far as I'm concerned.

He said it was for the "experience," but that man chose one of these older ladies and she sat so close to him she may as well have been inside of him. Mr Tony selected the front desk lady and they, as well as the unclaimed pros both looked at me again. The King of the Jungle gets to eat first, I guess.

It was so awkward looking a grown person in the face like that and shaking my head, but that's what I kept doing until they understood.

"Naw fam. I'm cool for real."

The extraneous ladies then left and it was the five of us. I can tell you this, I never pictured that I'd be the fifth wheel on a Korean norebang prostitution date, but I never imagined a lot of what my life has been.

I sat there and watched Mr Tony do his thing. He sang great, although the songs appeared to be Korean disco songs from the 80s. His lady also was hitting some notes y'all, even though I couldn't make out any of the words. Besides the sex I'm sure they eventually had, her voice was the biggest hit of the night.

Mitch looked conflicted for so long. Should he just do it? Would it be a story? Would he enjoy it? Would I judge him? I could see this man processing all these questions while some old Korean lady worked his hand up to his dick and was mashing it like an arcade button. I really thought he was doing some sort of performance art until his eyes rolled back and I couldn't keep looking at him. It was all so damn weird.

Finally he gave me a look that said fuck it, and the mashing ratcheted up to the point I had couldn't even glance to check in.

At one point, I was rapping the entire perfect lyrics to 'Forgot About Dre' and when I turned around everyone put their hands down real quick. That's all I know.

We never did deep dive into what happened that night after I went to bed. We just woke up in the hotel, gave one another a look, and got in a taxi. We probably never will.

CLAIM JUMPER

I often try, and fail, to explain just how ruthless college sports was socially. It was crazy how many Alphas were put into one talent pool and told to figure it out. I realized that I was not an alpha among alphas because I had no desire to compete with other dudes for women. In fact, I actively tried to go places other athletes were not so I wouldn't run into that issue. I thought I had kept my activities off the other athletes' radar.

I forget her name, but there was a girl I was interested in and we hung out one time on my birthday. A week later, I got a text from a homie saying that he was told that one of my teammates and a couple baseball guys had run a train on her and made sure to do anal. When I asked why he was telling me that, he said because they wanted me to know they got her first.

To this day I'll never understand that desire, but that's what athletes did. I'm sure I internalized that behavior and did it myself to someone else at some point. We were not good people all the time.

STEVEN V STEPHAN

In the spring of my junior year of high school, I was starting to blow up on the volleyball scene. So much so, that I was taking all sorts of unofficial visits to the Southern California schools. USC, UCLA, Pepperdine, and UCSB were all inviting me up for random sporting events, but UCLA seemed to have the most of them. I can't speak about now, but their recruiting machine hit different back then.

It was at that time that I took an unofficial to UCLA that had two events. The first event was a football game for hundreds of recruits. Admittedly, Men's Volleyball isn't the biggest sport, so they paired it with all the other sports for the same recruiting day. At this event I saw my first ever In N Out mobile truck and I was very impressed.

UCLA got money y'all.

I waited in line for a burger, and Matt Barnes walked by. He had a tattoo of the And 1 guy on his arm and it scared me.

He has a tattoo of something I'm barely comfortable with on a shirt.

When the game was over, we went back into Westwood for a basketball game on the same night. I think. It's murky if it was the same or next day. Either way, after we secured our tickets, my boy Alex and myself found our seats in the recruits section, behind the bench. I looked to my right, and Jaleel White was sitting next to us.

HOLY SHIT IT'S URKEL.

I played it cool and gave a nod. He was hype as hell to meet me until I told him I wasn't a basketball recruit.

"You sure?" He didn't believe me.

"Oh, no. I don't have the tattoo," I replied. Matt Barnes was still in my head.

"What? No man, I have a feeling you'll be back here next year."

When we got back to school, Alex and I must have told every kid we knew that Matt Barnes big-boyed me and Steve Erkel wished me luck. No one cared, save for Jordan Phillips. But we thought it was dope.

A year later, and we were back, but this time it was for basketball. Alex and I got into the locker room before the game and looked around. I remember thinking Dan Gadzuric was hella bigger than me, and I was trying hard to stand as tall as possible.

When we left the locker room, Lauren Woods walked by, and even with a kinda bent neck he was a foot taller than me. These dudes were massive. I felt like I was supposed to be there.

Alex and I took our seats and I looked to my right. It was Jaleel again!

"You might not remember me," I started, "But I-"

"Hell yea," Jaleel interrupted,"I remember you, Benson!"

HOLY SHIT I'VE ASCENDED. THESE HOES AIN'T LAURA.

"Oh yea word? Yea I almost forgot we ran into you here last year," I said as if this wasn't the moment I had been thinking about all coddamn 2001.

We then sat and talked with Jaleel about hoops for the next two hours. It was the first time I really felt like basketball made me more important, or something. Like there were real perks to this shit. Maybe Jordan Phillips was onto something all along.

STEVE

The first time I met Steve Fisher, I was loitering at the local Blockbuster. As a high school freshman, my days were super random. I played football but not basketball, and then I did track. I wasn't particularly good at any of the three, but that's besides the point.

Some days I would have practice, some days I wouldn't, and I think my mom never really understood the difference. Maybe she did and she was just busy. Either way, some days I would spend hours waiting for her to pick me up from school.

Many of these days were spent hanging around the Carmel Valley Rec trying to play other kids in 5 on 5, or hanging around the Del Mar Heights shopping center. It was a rather unique shopping center given that it was very nice (designed by and for people with money). But it also had a mcDonalds that still had the 50's style tiling inside and a full size Dinosaur statue thing, wearing sunglasses, and the the Red Robin - AMC Theater combination was a teenage dream.

Anyways, this site also had a Blockbuster. People forget that Blockbuster used to sell soda, candy, and games and whatnot, especially in its last days, so I would just loiter and look at movie covers. That was my afternoon a lot of days.

And then one day, Steve Fisher appeared. He just looked at me. I was all of 6'3", and he looked me up and down. He gave a small nod and went about his business. I did not go about my business. I took this as a sign that I was being scouted by the real coaches who knew what was really good. That was obviously not accurate.

I saw Steve Fisher in the same blockbuster a year later. I was now 6'7." He remembered me. At the time, I figured he just saw potential, and that's probably true, but I now also can tell when a boy has a basketball body he hasn't grown into yet. Looking back I can tell he could sense that in me. This time he spoke.

"How's the season coming along?"

"Good," I lied. I still wasn't on the team, but volleyball was promising.

"Ok well I'll be looking for you."

I told you assholes he was scouting me. I don't care what Bryce said.

I saw him a couple times that year. It was pretty much the same. He was always so damn nice.

The next time I saw Steve Fisher, Torrey Pines was playing in a summer tournament hosted by San Diego State. I hadn't even played a varsity game, but I was on the roster for the summer. Fisher and his son sat court side to watch us, the number one team in San Diego, and I was hyped. I remember I got a fast break dunk and was bragging about it to everyone on the squad as we ate sandwiches between games.

"Steve Fisher saw me dunk," I said as I was untying my shoes.

"Rod. You've never even dunked in the half court," Ryan Cooper said, just to be a dick.

He was right, though. Those guys weren't there to see me.

The next time I met Steve Fisher was pre-game. We were lining up to play SDSU at the Cox Pavilion, my junior year at Cal. My mom, her husband, and Russell (my childhood mentor) all made it out. It was like I had finally come home to show San Diego that I was now that dude. Steve shook my hand and I think we both had a moment of

Nice. Fancy running into you here.

He didn't say much over the years, but he didn't have to. Every time I saw him at that Blockbuster, he really did give me just enough inspiration to keep trying.

Thanks, Steve.

NOW YOU SEE ME

I used to consider myself the best basketball player in Vancouver, Canada. I'd spent considerable time there in my off-seasons, because Sharon is a local, so I would fly directly from Seoul into Vancouver, breathe that sweet air, and then just chill around town while she went to work.

On occasion, we'd head to Kits Beach, one of the few beaches in Canada that has a California feel. It's got all sorts of volleyball, tennis, and basketball courts in plain view and all of them are in use. Because it rains so often, people flood the beach on sunny days and soak in both the water and the athletics.

One day Mike, a volunteer with Kits Fest, saw me walking around, watching the basketball, but not playing. I used to be very careful about where I played in the offseason.

"Why aren't you playing, big fella?" Mike asked. It's such a common question.

"Oh. Ha. I don't play."

I was used to lying. It made things easier. Better to leave someone confused than spend three minutes explaining the nuance of overseas basketball.

"You don't have to lie to me, Rod Benson. I know who you are."

He explained that people were talking about my being in town. I did play a little at the YMCA, but those games were trash. I hated them. In general, pick up games are ass for someone like me.

They're only so many possible outcomes, most of them bad. I either get injured or in a fight, oftentimes both go hand in hand. I completely dominate, to which people respond with anger. They ask why I would even choose to play with such low level competition. If they had my height, of course they'd also be dominant. Or, if I play poorly, win or lose, it doesn't matter. I'm too big to be trash. My entire career is now invalid.

Both cases in point, I was once bullshitting in a game at LA Fitness in Hollywood. I wasn't playing poorly, but I had developed a lazy game that allowed me to avoid fighting and injury. Van Lathan from TMZ was there playing and watching, which wasn't unusual. He was there often. On a particular play, someone hit me in the face and I got upset. It almost turned into a fight, but instead, I channeled my abilities. I completely took over, dominating the game in every way. After the game Van came up to me looking confused.

"Oh you can really play. Like you're good. I thought you were trash before, no offense."

None taken.

Anyways, in Vancouver, guys were not only smaller and less talented, they were just whinier than pick up dudes in LA. They aren't bums like that. It's not like there's just no talent up there, it's just that something about LA basketball is just different. I could feel the bitch-assness of the game up there.

So I'd get into pickup games at the Vancouver YMCA and just play lazy, yell and complain, and eke out dumb victories that no one cared about while Sharon sat on the sidelines. I'd play hungover, halfheartedly, and always win. I never felt challenged, so there was a point where I started saying (and believing) that I was the best basketball player in the city of Vancouver. I may have been.

"Yea. I guess that is me," I replied to Mike, who was looking up to me through thick glasses.

"I'd like you to play in Kist Fest. It's the best basketball on the West Coast (of Canada). You'll have a real challenge and the event is very fun." Mike said a lot more than this.

He's quite long winded sometimes, but he's passionate. He repeated this plea summer after summer from 2016, until now. He calls me every year.

I'd been retired for a year when I finally agreed to play in the Kits Fest tournament. Mike felt that I would be the perfect ringer, the next in a long line of ringers, to help bring home the chip for the actual Kits Beach team. There were many teams that entered, but the Kits Beach team was supposed to be the best in the country.

I wasn't in good shape when we played, but I was still very good at basketball. It was a little tough on my chest, though, because I hadn't really touched a ball since April 2018 and it was now August 2019. The team let me sub in and out as I wished on that first day so I didn't injure myself or burn out. I was really kind of going through the motions, scoring at will even if it was against the lowest seeded team in the tournament. We were the first.

On the second day of the tournament it was raining and I was sore. The normally beautiful scenery of Kits Beach was hastily replaced by the dry indoor auxiliary gym of the University of British Columbia. It was not dope.

When the game started, the other team had a clear plan to foul. They had nobody over 6'6" and here I was 6'10". It made sense. The football strategy never stops.

My teammates were starting to fold because the strategy was working, slowing us down just enough to make a tired team have to work harder. In prior games, I took these fouls and played through them with ease, but my fatigue was setting in after a year off. I didn't have the energy to play through that kind of contact. These games didn't matter to me, so I was just going to take a seat. That's when Sharon's dad, Nick, walked in.

Nick and I had been building a relationship for a few years at this point. He's a serious man and incredibly smart. Dude is actually a seismic engineer of the highest regard, flying the globe teaching people how to be better prepared for earthquakes, and working on impossible projects that always seem to need to save money and resources. Yea, we've had some interesting chats. But Nick had never seen me compete. He had only ever heard about it.

See, another thing about Sharon's dad is that he was still a world class athlete. He played collegiate volleyball and essentially never stopped. He still plays beach volleyball multiple days a week and competes in world masters championships, often medalling as a group of 60-somethings.

I don't know what it is about the father of the girlfriend, but I always wanted him to respect my grind. I wanted him to see me play for real. He knew I was good at basketball, but he didn't *know*, you know? He didn't know my fire. He never saw the games. He wasn't following me on Instagram, so he couldn't see the highlights. All he knew was that his daughter was dating a relatively safe seeming negro from LA. He would never say that, but after a while, I felt I had something to prove to this man.

When Daddy Nick showed up to watch, a switch flipped within me. I hadn't even played competitively in over a year so I forgot what was laying dormant. It was like I went Grimy all over again. I became a rage monster — the dude who slaps people and rips his jersey off and leads the league in technicals.

I was muscling dudes out of the way. Cussing fools out. Rebounding and blocking shots at will. Screaming and dunking and all that.

On one play, I got an offensive rebound, went back up through multiple points of contact, and finished the and one. I screamed and beat my chest. It was the kind of celebration that makes inexperienced refs confused about if they should call a tech, but they don't want to ruin themoment. It was just like the old days. I looked over at Mr Nick.

NOW YOU SEE ME.

We won by a wide margin, in the end. Afterwards, it was just the three of us, me, him and Sharon and I felt like something had changed. I don't know if he expected me to flip like that. I felt like he was studying me. I had never even raised my voice around him, let alone been more than a tired hungover visitor.

But now there was a new respect there. He now knew what I was capable of. It wasn't about basketball. It was that I was capable of doing whatever was necessary to achieve a goal, and maybe that's something a father wants to see in the partner of his daughter.

Or maybe it was all in my head and that's how motivation works. It had been a while.

THE LONG GAME

I once pretended to be friends with a guy for a whole season. We went out and I would buy his drinks. I'd comment on his posts. I'd hype him up and teach him the ropes. This was all a lie.

The first game of the playoffs, I spent the whole game literally taking one finger and poking him in the side. It wasn't a foul but it was annoying as all hell.

"I thought you were the homie bruh" he finally yelled out in frustration.

No. I played the long game.

Dongbu in 4.

DIZZY ROOSTER

When I was drafted by Austin in 2006, everyone was happy for me. Everyone kept telling me about its political history. They kept making sure I knew that I was headed to the 'Berkeley of the South.' Whoever dubbed it that was lying.

"Keep Austin Weird" they would say, as if one white guy in a tutu was weird. Austin was not weird.

When I actually got to Austin, it wasn't what I expected whatsoever. Outside of the chorus of folks educating me on the city, I had already learned a great deal from The Real World: Austin. The Real World, however, really only showed the cast at their house and a couple of bars. I didn't expect a replica of the US Capitol building, traffic everywhere, and blatant racism in every direction. If this was Berkeley, it was a fucked up version with more live music.

Coincidentally, the NBA had just instituted the famous dress code. It was an odd time to do so, because they just dropped it on us and we had no money for clothing upgrades. In a matter of days, the NBA went from pregame fits of Sean Jean velour suits to slacks and polos league-wide. That was the NBA.

We, in the D-League, were working with shoestring budgets. I could afford one pair of slimmer jeans and a couple very boxy button ups from Men's Fashion Depot. I paired this with some dusty old dress shoes. They were all I had.

My team definitely let me have it about the shoes. There was a JB Smoove stand up special (you can google it) at the time talking about horrible shoes and my teammates used to play it on the bus, all laughing at the part that reminded them of my busted ass church kicks.

"Shoes so turnt over he gotta lay down to put them on!"

"Rod and them DAMN BOOTS!"

This led to an interesting set of circumstances. I essentially had three wardrobes: a social one, a basketball one, and an Austin one. The social wardrobe consisted of shit I would wear anywhere at any time. These were mostly T-Shirts, a decent pair of jeans, and vans. I actually dressed pretty well with no restrictions, broke or not.

It was the other two wardrobes that used to piss me off. The one I had to wear to games was ass, and the one I had to wear to bars was stupid. I learned very quickly that in Austin, every bar had a dress code. They fully lied on The Real World. Not only was there a dress code, it was obviously a very racist one. The bars, yes basic ass bars, were incredibly segregated. Dizzy Rooster, the bar frequented most often on Real World, was a white bar for sure. White women galore. Coyote Ugly was the same. Both had strict dress codes and no black people.

If I wanted to attend one of these bars, I would need to essentially dress up like a white window salesman. Tucked in polo, very tight jeans or slacks, and some trainers. This was just to get IN to Austin bars. The shitty part was that all the other patrons would be in cutoff jeans and boots and shit. There was one time I argued with the bouncer because he said my pants were too baggy, while some frat guys without shirts and wearing flip flops walked right past me and inside. The segregation was palpable.

I'd go to the games dressed like I was there with my grandmother for Sunday Service, rocking loose fitting dress clothes and dirty shoes. I only wore that *nice* outfit to walk the 45 seconds from the car into the Austin Convention Center, holding a backpack full of window salesman bar clothes that I'd have to change after the game. I learned quickly that even that bullshit church outfit, which was good enough for David Stern, was not good enough for Dizzy Rooster.

All of this had a horrible effect on my non-existent checking account. My entire $400 budget was spent on making sure I was allowed to leave my house, stylistically. After a while I stopped going to the white bars altogether.

I'm not mad at the dress code, though. Not even two years later and every team in the NBA had an in-house stylist, helping players to look their best. The polos quickly became fancy leather jackets and silk suits and once big name black designers got into the mix, the state of men's fashion changed forever.

I've said for years that David Stern had a bigger impact on men's fashion that Louis Vuitton. Just wish he could do something about my damn boots.

A-A-RON

My junior year at Cal was the most fun because I had really started to find my way athletically and socially. It was the year Richard Midgley and I lived on frat row, so the party game went to another level. This was confirmed when I tried to throw my first ever party and it ended up being buck wild. The entire women's basketball team was gigging to Ying Yang Twins and broke my futon. They later dubbed it 'Rod Fest.'

This was also the year that the football team was making waves. Aaron Rodgers, who had taken over at QB, was on the preseason Heisman list and was currently living up to it. I had had a couple good games to start the season and was building hype. We would pass each other near Sather Gate.

"Heisman!" I would say to him.

"Naismith," he would say back lying, but it was nice.

I really didn't know him well beyond that. I didn't really know many football players very well. They generally were unkind to me, and I'm sure I was way too goofy for them. Either way, I just didn't know many, and I certainly wouldn't say Aaron and I were besties. But we were both out here doing it, and that counted for something.

One night there was an invite party. These were parties thrown by sororities that required "bids," often used as a ticket to board a chartered bus from Berkeley to San Francisco. Upon arrival in SF, the girls could break the house rules because they were in a different zip code. I think.

These were heavily attended by athletes because these were the only available women who cared about athletics maybe in the whole city. For real. It was slim Pickens compared to other schools. Berkeley, and a lot of its social working, boiled down to one thing: numbers. I don't know them exactly, so these are approximations.

30K UNDERGRADS TOTAL.

15K OF THOSE ARE HERE FROM ANOTHER COUNTRY AND DON'T SPEAK ENGLISH NOR CARE TO GO TO PARTIES

8K OF THE REMAINING PEOPLE ARE FROM HERE AND SPEAK ENGLISH AND STILL DON'T CARE TO GO TO PARTIES

3500 OF THE REMAINING PEOPLE ARE MEN

OF THE REMAINING 3500 WOMEN, HOW MANY ARE ATTRACTIVE DEPENDS ON YOUR SENSIBILITIES.

OF THOSE, MOST BELONGED TO FOUR SORORITIES OR THEY PLAYED SPORTS.

Simple math, right? Because of the numbers, all these bloodthirsty athletes were dying for an invite party. Where else could we get that level of aggregation?

For me, I usually avoided invite parties. Clay, JGant, and I purposefully went to the parties less attended. Maybe it wasn't the 'hottest' choice, but it was better than going out with 200 people who will purposefully steal your chick.

But I was starting to feel myself now that I was on Aaron Rodgers' 'Naismith Watch' list. I was starting to meet women in real life, not just on BlackPlanet.com. It seemed like the logical move to go to this party.

I don't remember the ride there, but I remember arriving to the Broadway club. It was small and hot, like most venues in those days.

When I got in, everything was a blur. I used to arrive at the party pretty drunk, so this was normal.

What wasn't normal was that Arron Rodgers was there. It was right after football season, so he was getting pretty loose. The entire football team was. They actually were nice people now that they didn't have the weight of college football on their shoulders. Our team was good. These were future pro-bowlers.

Aaron saw me and didn't hesitate. He was holding one bottle and two women. Boss shit. He handed me the bottle and told me to drink it. I fucking pounded that shit. Aaron Rodgers needed to see that I was the sheriff around these parts, vodka-wise. And that he did. The memory gets fuzzier and fuzzier, but I feel like he just kept handing me drinks.

Next thing I remember was that on the way out, gunshots rang out. Everyone was shook. I hid behind a women's basketball player and then gaslit her by telling her I protected her. I was so drunk she probably just laughed at me.

My next memory is being on the bus much earlier than everyone else. I didn't feel well at all. I looked up for the bus driver. No one was there. It was just me, so I went to the bathroom to try to throw up. A minute later, someone was pounding on the door, I said nothing. They then opened it, looked at me and said "oh."

My next memory was very loud banging on the door. I opened it. It was the bus driver.

"Thank God man. When are we leaving? I'm not ok. I was drinking with Aaron. Grodgers."

"Dude get the fuck off the bus! We're in Berkeley."

I stood up in a pile of who knows what and looked out onto the bus. It was totally empty.

"FUCK OFF THE BUS!" the driver shouted at me, startling me enough to stumble.

I exited and looked around frat row. It was completely dead. That was weird considering the size of the party. I guess it was 4am. The driver had been trying to wake me up for an hour. I stumbled home, just then noticing that my shirt was ripped.

How Sway?

There's a lot of things I can blame for that night, but I will blame no one more than myself. JK I blame Aaron Rodgers.

THE

AGENT.

Got a law degree, but you'd rather spend time on a different court?

Is there something exciting about negotiating deals with Turkish authorities to get your guy home? How much informaton do you have to leak to the media? So much?

You should get your Ari Gold on an become an agent! Your babysitting skills wil be put to the test as you fund, feed, bail out and look after grown men! The best part is they wont respect you for it!

Better keep the deals comin so your player stays happy!

DD
DIFFERENT
DUDE™

EMAILS FROM BILL 7

From: BILL

To: RIDICULOUS UPSIDE

Sent: 4/15/2010 8:46:43 A.M. Eastern Daylight Time

Subj: Re: Rod

Ridiculous: You know I am your biggest fan. On Rod, and feel free to use whatever you want. Please note the use of ridiculous whenever possible.

NBA personnel people have a very difficult job. I respect what they do. One of the most ridiculous things to me is how few guys make judgments with such little information on draftees, on players. They may see them once, twice, on a good day, on a bad day. They do not get a feel for them as people. Research & development should be a much larger part of their budget but is not and that is why they fail at times. That they are correct as often as they are is remarkable considering how little they spend in this area.

Having said that, on Rod Benson, they could not be more wrong. He is an NBA player. Period. I independently spoke to 5 D League coaches and all of them said he was the best center in the League but the NBA guys are "scared of him" or "think he's strange."

In his first year, with the great Dave Joerger coaching him, they won a championship and he had five blocks in the Championship game. In the second year, he led his team to a divisional crown and led the D League in rebounding. In his third year, he returned from France to find a logjam in Dakota. Thankfully, he was moved to Reno. He got there and they won 10 of their last 12 or something like that and they missed out on the playoffs the last day. This year, he was hurt early but once he got healthy, they got hot again, made a trade for the right people and soared into the playoffs.

They almost beat RGV and RGV was frightened enough to bring back a player who should be the logo for the quintessential D League player, Mike Harris, to help vanquish Reno and Rod, who only went 26 & 22, 29 & 18 and in his bad game, 21 & 11. If someone can rebound in the D League, they can rebound in the NBA.

. . .

Bottom line is what is scary about Rod, that he is the D League's all-time leading rebounder, wins everywhere he goes, is more versatile than any of the other big men called up, had the highest defensive ratings by Synergy and is extremely well thought of by coaches like Joerger and Jay Humphries, for instance. Add Indiana to that list after Rod was with them in camp. And, off the court, he is smart, loyal, funny, looks you in the eye, never causes an ounce of trouble, can carry a serious discussion with you on health care but happened to write a ridiculous blog that poked fun of himself a lot. He does not even write the blog anymore. The good news for blog readers is that now, if he has to use his passport, they may read more of his prose. Had he stayed here, he would have kept his thoughts to himself.

Here is a final Rod story. At the D League Showcase in Boise this year, Rod had just fouled out on two pretty questionable calls early in the 4th. He went to the bench, angry, disgusted, threw his headband to the ground hard. A scout whose NBA team was having a problem with one of its players, said this to me about Rod. "He really has to control his emotions." I said to him, "I am sorry that he cares." You can make any excuse you want for keeping a guy out and that was the best one.

Ultimately, I think this is where the NBA fails. Because of their lack of personnel and because they fear for their own security, they make the safe selection instead of picking up the phone to Joerger or Humphries and hearing how much he helped their teams win, which is the only thing that should matter.

SAT GPA

As a sophomore in High School, I wasn't really on any teams. I was just a kid who went to class and went home. If I had any chance to be cool, my mom ruined that the day she signed up to teach there. I'd arrive with her in the morning and leave with her at night.

Not that it mattered. No girls liked me and no one invited me to hang out or to parties. The one time I was invited to a party, some kids called me a nigger and told me to leave.

I had picked up playing Pokemon at an unhealthy level, spending most of my days linking cord to cord with the autistic kids in my moms special ed class because we were the only ones out there raising level 100 beasts organically without rare candy. Them boys was wrong strong.

I was on JV basketball, but I didn't have a jersey. They did this just to make kids feel good, but really it was to make the parents happy. In a school full of very wealthy white kids, leaving someone out was a no-no. I had a jersey because Timmy had one and Timmy had a future. My season was reduced to showing up, doing the pregame stuff, and then putting on street clothes and sitting in the stands with the families brave enough to sit through white JV basketball.

I was 6'7" and could now dunk, so it always looked awkward when our team would run out and I would put on my Sony Discman and take a seat. I knew this was odd optically, so on occasion, I would get up at half time and do a few dunks in street clothes. The whole gym would stop and watch, then I would sit my sweaty ass back down in the stands thinking I had accomplished something.

One day I was sitting and watching, but there were no dunks to be had. I had broken my wrist snowboarding and my family didn't have healthcare. So I sat up there with the cardboard sling the Ski Patrol had put on my wrist, watching the game like this was all normal. Everyone did think it was normal, except for Jeff Harper.

Jeff was an AAU coach who was at the game waiting for the Varsity game to start. I learned, by listening in, that he coached my best friend Alex on said AAU team. I didn't understand how. Alex was good, but he was sitting next to me in the stands without a jersey. Not only that, Alex was as Jewish as they came – down to the fro, and Jeff was a shit talking negro from Ohio. How the hell was he on that AAU team?

"Nigga! WHAT?!"

Jeff's yell interrupted my eavesdropping.

"Snowboarding?!"

He was talking to me? I guess Alex had told him how I hurt myself.

"Uh. Yea. I was attempting a 36– "

"Nigga no. This is what I hate about Torrey Pines. They got 7 footers out here brainwashed and snowboarding," he declared for all the scared Karens just trying to handle their orange slices.

I'm only 6'7" and I'm good at snowboarding, guy.

"I'm only 6'7" and I'm good at snowboarding, guy," I said confidently.

"NIGGA THEY EVEN TOOK HIS VOICE!"

I don't remember the rest, but he was upset at everything about me. He hated how I dressed, walked, talked, and most importantly, he hated that I was in the stands watching basketball with a snow-boarding injury.

"We need to get you to Southeast."

"Southeast San Diego?"

It was weird that I had never heard someone say it without the 'San Diego' at the end. It was another tell.

"This nigga. I swear. We gonna make you a basketball player."

It took a year, but the following spring, after a volleyball season that saw me become a top national prospect, I got in the car with Alex and headed down to Southeast San Diego. The connection, I learned, was that Alex and his other Jewish bestie Avi had grown up together. Avi is half black and his mom, who had converted, was cousins with Jeff. So Jeff and Avi and been working together for years, with Avi sometimes choosing to play for Jeff when he wasn't playing with the big name teams.

Avi was also a rising star on the Torrey Pines team. He was good. Alex may have just been a combo package to keep Avi around the AAU team, or so I had to assume. Because of this, a couple other Jewish kids and the homie Ryan Cooper all joined the team over time. I was the last one.

So oddly, the San Diego Cougars, the team I was now joining, was a mix of 12 black kids from the hood, four jewish kids from the beach, and me. It was weird right away.

From jump I was a target. It wasn't in a bad way, but everyone could see what I couldn't see: I was so far from being in a basketball mind that this was going to take some work. A lot of fucking work.

First it was the running. It was more running than I had ever thought a human could experience. It was miserable. What was worse was that Jeff was unkind about it. He'd make me run extra laps and call me a bitch in front of everyone. He would line me up and not let me jump, then tell people to try to dunk on me. Repeatedly.

My teammates, all black kids with their own set of issues, challenged me every day, looking for ways to expose me. Some days it would be about my skill, others about my language, and others about just how I was a bitch. Every day was brutal. And then the games started.

It was an odd time, going from not playing JV to being thrown into games with the best players in the country. Back then guys existed purely on word of mouth. Guys like Evan Burns and Tyson Chandler were out there. Omar Wilkes was out there. DeAngelo Collins was out there. We played all of them and got absolutely destroyed. Melo's team, Baltimore Select, beat us by 55.

I would finish games with stat lines of 2 points and 1 rebound in 15 minutes and have positive takeaways. How could I not? I didn't even think I was supposed to be there. Jeff didn't agree.

"Y'all," he would start, "we let them niggas get in our ass. They beat y'all by 35. 35? Y'all could have won that shit if Rod wasn't out there playing like a bitch."

I would sit there on random lawns at community colleges across Southern California and Nevada just getting reamed. He would tell me to hit people and I would refuse.

"No nigga. Hit people. Go back to Torrey Pines and kick Frank in the balls. Kick that nigga! Punch coach Cherry in the face. I don't give a fuck!"

WHY IS HE ONLY YELLING AT ME? I HAD 4 POINTS.

But also, I weirdly agreed with him. It's not like Torrey Pines kids liked me. What was worse was that at home games the TP kids would chant stuff like "SAT, GPA, You're gonna work for us someday" when we played black schools.

I couldn't be mad at Jeff for trying to get me to see the truth.

One day, we were in a tournament called "Adidas Best of the Summer" at Loyola Marymount. A ton of top talent was there, including Chris Bosh. We had just taken an L and here we were again, sitting on the lawn.

"This nigga Rod LOOK like Chris Bosh, but he play like if Chris Bosh lost both his legs in the war."

I sat there and took it. Same as always. But I do remember thinking that I did kinda look like Chris Bosh. At least I did from a distance.

The next game, against some Canadian team called the Jr Trojans, against all odds, I had 37 points. 18 of them came on dunks. I don't even know what happened. I just played better than I ever had before. I wish I had some explanation like I was hyped because of the yelling. I wasn't. I didn't have Michael's secret stuff. The team wasn't bad. There was literally no answer. After the game, which we won, we sat on the lawn.

"Marcus. This nigga Marcus didn't come to play today..."

Jeff didn't say shit to me. He actually never checked me again. He didn't have to. I was now good at basketball. Every game we played I had 20 plus and we won a lot of the games. To this day I still can't explain it. One minute I was bad, the next I was good.

I came into my Senior year at Torrey Pines with 5 Division One scholarship offers. It was wild because I wasn't even on the team. It was assumed that I would be on Varsity, maybe even that I would contribute, but no one expected me to walk back into that school as the man. This caused a lot of problems.

See, TP was already #1 in San Diego and had just won the CIF championship. This was part of why I wasn't on the team. I wasn't needed, really. The same five guys had played together since 7th grade at Earl Warren. They had that special white guy basketball chemistry that meant they could out-strategy anyone. And all of this was Coach Cherry's doing. The man could coach his ass off. To this day I have not met a stronger basketball mind at the high school level. Adding some black kid nobody liked 'just because' was unnecessary.

But I walked in and was good. So good that heads began to turn. After all, I was now one of two guys with D1 offers. When the starting PG went down, I was slotted into the starting line up for the opening game of the season and I had something like 22 and 10. This caused a stir because now the media was expecting me to keep starting. The other parents, however, took exception.

I get why. The guys had literally all been together for years and they had been winners. To alleviate this, Cherry called a meeting and told us all that we would have six starters. Each guy would come off the bench on a rotating basis. It seemed to be the fairest option. It worked, too, until we got to my turn.

We were playing in our own tournament, the Torrey Pines Prep Classic, which had top teams from around the country and scouts from every college and NBA team. You could still go straight to the league back then so the scouts in attendance were in abundance. I remember sitting next to a scout from Boston who was there to see Evan Burns. The hype back then was real.

In the first game of the tournament, against our local rivals La Costa Canyon, I had like 30 and 20. The next day I was on the front page of the Sports Section with the headline "At 6' 10 1/2", Benson's Outgrown Volleyball." After that, the rotation died. So did our team chemistry. That's another story.

The next day, I woke up annoyed. My mom had been on the phone for over an hour already and it was loud. I got up to ask her if there was some sort of emergency. Why the hell would Grandma keep calling this early on a Sunday? She put up a finger to signal for me to wait and be quiet so I did.

"That was some man from a school called Wake Forest asking about you. I already told him you weren't going," she said as she hung up the phone.

"WHAT?!" I was still waking up. "WHAT?!"

"Oh yea. I've been getting calls all morning. Since you're going to Yale, I told Kansas no. I told some other guys from Texas no."

I was so happy and confused I didn't know what to do with myself. But I wasn't actually mad.

I sat by the phone as it rang all day non stop. I must have taken 200 calls that day. I took every single one. I had never been given a direct reward for that level of work before. To this day, that was one of the best days of my life. I had made it. I was going to be the man. I was finally about to live the life I had seen on TV.

The next week I was rated as the #3 Center prospect on the West Coast and the #1 late signing prospect in the country. I ended up signing with Cal and heading off to college in July.

"I don't know who's up there," Jeff said in one of our last games before I left for The Bay, "but kick-punch them in the face, too."

RETIREMENT

The day I actually, finally, retired for good was the least pleasing of them all. I stood alone, broke, ashamed, and confused about how I did it all wrong. Basketball, its ideologies, expectations, hype, everything; it all faded away. I know that people go through this in all walks of life, but oddly enough, only athletes get that part talked about like the person was too dumb to figure it out. I suppose I was. The joke was finally over and I was the butt of it. I buried my head in my hands and cried for a good hour.

If I wanted to be anything else in life that had value, I had to go back to who I was before the slap. Sure, the slap had provided the catalyst for my entire career, but it was always an overlay. 'Rod Benson' as he became known, was made up; he was always designed to have an expiration date. I had just forgotten.

I had built overlay on top of overlay in a desperate attempt to first fit in, and then to become the athlete I was supposed to be. As each layer peeled back, eventually I realized I'm still the scared boy holding onto something that gave me joy that day when I was 6 years old and learned that a basketball was not for kicking.

In the end, basketball connected me to the world. It became my dad, my best friend, and my sounding board and I needed that for so long.

Life was hard and frightening, and basketball gave me a cheat code to cut through the malarkey and become great.

But the day I truly let basketball go was the day I started to actually become great. I found that kid, still sitting in the backseat hoping his dad would turn around. I found the 8th grader ashamed that he couldn't afford shorts and shoes. I found this college freshman, confused why all the girls liked his teammates when he was trying so hard to get their attention. I found the guy who had just cleaned up after all these people in his house to find a woman he was in love with masturbating and insulting him. I finally found the person Sharon always begged me to share with her every time she would plead with me to let her in. I could see why now. I didn't know what 'in' was.

I found all these versions of myself hiding behind basketball like it was shielding my life force itself. Every time I felt like the journey was painful, it was because it was actually just painful to the real me hiding beneath; a Horcrux desperately afraid to be exposed.

Basketball protected me. It held me when no one else would. It gave me a chance to prove my worth. Basketball took me everywhere and gave me perspective. It was the most necessary vice I've ever had, because it also held me back.

Too much basketball, not enough love.

But that's really it now. I'll never play basketball again for money, and if I did I'd likely lose. I don't have that spark anymore. No, not the spark to play, but the spark to compete; the kind of spark it takes to slap a grown man in the face and make a life of it. Never again.

DIFFERENT DUDE

On the fourth of July, 2009, I was posted outside of Lake Tahoe, bored. I'm not gonna lie, I had gone up there with Madison to visit some of her friends and we were just doing the most boring white shit imaginable. 'Tanning' and 'sipping beer' were the activities for the weekend. I didn't know it back then, but as an appeasing person, I said yes to this weekend thinking I could adapt to any situation. I couldn't.

Eventually, to stop from going crazy, I snatched a book that someone had just put down. Thinking I wouldn't make it a quarter of the way through before days end, I started reading. I think I started reading almost sarcastically; as if the book itself would show people just how bored I was. That plan didn't work at all. By day's end I was fully hooked on "Twilight."

The timing here was important, because two days later I had to fly into Vegas for the NBA Summer league and I was by no means finished with the series by the time I arrived. I was firmly into "New Moon" as the time approached for my first practice with the Rockets.

I went down to the trainers room to get taped, and while there I read the ballad of Jacob and Bella the entire time. I'm sure I didn't even look up from the book to introduce myself.

I got on the team bus and kept reading as the guys walked past me. By this point in my career, my reputation as an outlier preceded me a bit. I remember Chase Budinger walking by and shaking his head. They all did. Four other guys and a coach walked by and said out loud:

"Ayo this man Rod is different."

"Y'all seeing this? Man's is different bro."

And my favorite: "Nigga Rod gay."

They couldn't understand how I could be into anything they weren't into, and I couldn't understand why Bella was so concerned with Jacob's age when it was clear that he was building emotional maturity. Sure, he was now 6'5" after gaining his powers, but his mental growth was even larger. Could she not see that he was always there for her, warm and comforting, during her most trying times? That she wouldn't have to leave her family to be with him? That she could stop hurting Charlie?

Could Bella not see that Edward always *tried* to protect her and never actually listened to her needs? Could she not see that he was a 109 year old predator? That everything she loved about him came from the fact that he spent decades going to high school over and over, sharpening his skills? That all the poetry and books and everything were just common knowledge for a man in the 1940's? That he can't be considered old fashioned if he's just old? Like maybe he didn't even really know how to read minds, he just had so much experience with high school women, he knew what they were thinking instinctively? Why couldn't Bel-

"Bro!"

I forgot where I was. Someone had sat down next to me. Summer league buses were always so full. Too many guys.

"What's good?" I asked.

"You've been staring out the window with your mouth open for hella long."

"Yea? I do that."

He looked me up and down. We were meeting for the first time.

"You a different dude, man."

WORDS AINT ENOUGH VOL 1.

DD
DIFFERENT DUDE™

WE DIDNT CHOOSE THE THUG LIFE

MY FIRST PHOTO OF A DUNK

12 DAYS IN DR

CONTEXT FROM 2008

CHAIN HANG TO MY DANGALANG

IT'S TOP LEFT FOR ME

SHE NEVER REACHED OUT

THEM RENO BOYS

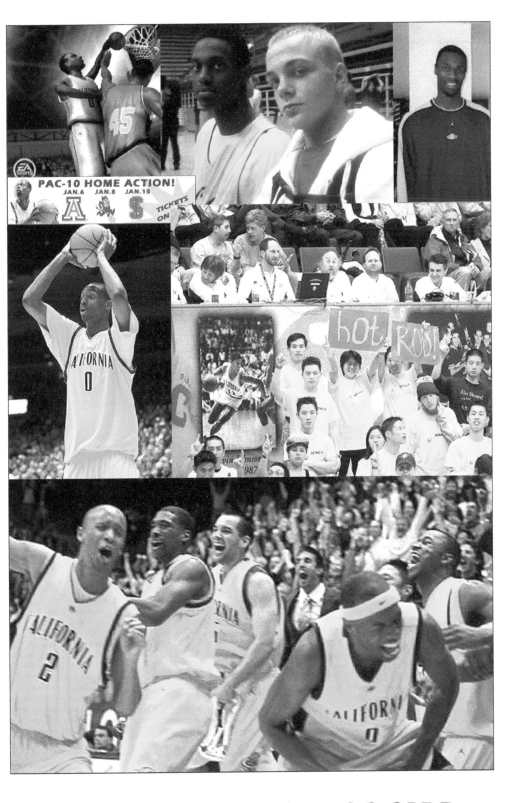

JUST A PRODUCT OF DOC CARR

ONCE I GOT PAID IT WAS OVER

THE SNOWBOARDER

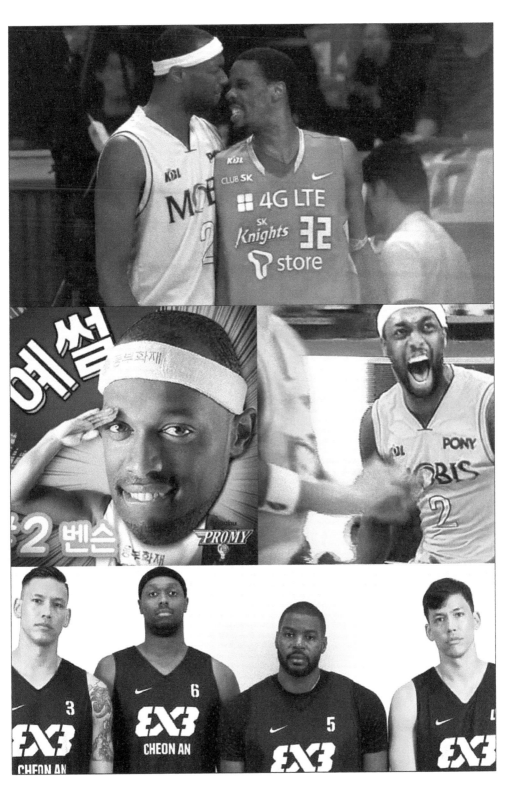

EAGERLY AWAITING BIBIMBAP

I DID PLAY HARD THO

IT WAS A MOVEMENT

Torrey Pines' Rod Benson interrupts a shot by an unsuspecting La Costa Canyon player. *Eduardo Contreras / Union-Tribune*

At 6-10½, Benson's outgrown volleybal

THEY DIDN'T PUT HIS NAME

ABOUT THE AUTHOR

Rod Benson is a professional basketball player turned fine artist, writer, and improv comedian who grew up in San Diego, CA. After four years playing NCAA D1 Basketball at UC Berkeley, he began two careers: one as a professional basketball player, and the other as a writer.

In basketball, Benson started in the D-League in Austin, TX, and eventually played for teams in North Dakota, Reno, Dominican Republic, New Jersey, Indianapolis, France, Puerto Rico, Taiwan, and Korea. He won championships in North Dakota (2007), DR (2010), and Korea (2012, 2013, 2014). He was named an All Star and all league several times, and in 2008, he set a then D-League record of 28 rebounds while adding 28 points in the same game. He has also held the offensive rebounding record (11) and still sits fourth on the D-League's all time rebounding list (1656), despite leaving the league in 2010. Benson also broke Korea's all time rebounding record (5600) and consecutive double doubles (32) respectively.

Off the court, Benson started his blog called "Too Much Rod Benson" in 2006, which quickly led to a blog of the same name on DraftExpress. After that, he signed to Yahoo! to create "Ball Don't Lie" alongside JE Skeets, Yahoo!'s first ever sports blog. Following Yahoo!, he added credits from SLAM, HoopsHype, and others, until he retired from basketball in 2018.

Today, Rod has made art and writing his full time endeavors. Benson's artwork, which he produces under his middle name, ZSORRYON, has been shown in national and international galleries from Los Angeles to New York to South Korea and has been featured in various magazines and newspapers. His pieces can also be seen in ABC's "The Rookie," on NBC's "GRAND CREW," and in the homes of various NBA players, celebrities, in movie studios, and collectors of black art.

Outside of the gallery, Benson produces countless street art projects challenging people's idea of what belongs and what doesn't in public spaces.

He also signed with SFGATE in 2021 as a regular columnist, Bear Insider as a podcaster and writer, and he started "HOOP STORIES," a web series detailing funny stories from his career.

Rod Benson is always finding ways to tell stories in new and different ways, be it via writing, art, or sport.

Milton Keynes UK
Ingram Content Group UK Ltd.
UKHW020224301123
433460UK00016B/271/J